My Life and Experiences
in the
Entertainment World

by

Mertis John

DORRANCE PUBLISHING CO., INC.
PITTSBURGH, PENNSYLVANIA 15222

All Rights Reserved
Copyright © 2001 by Mertis John
No part of this book may be reproduced or transmitted
in any form or by any means, electronic or mechanical,
including photocopying, recording, or by any information
storage and retrieval system without permission in
writing from the publisher.

ISBN # 0-8059-5040-0
Printed in the United States of America

First Printing

For information or to order additional books, please write:
Dorrance Publishing Co., Inc.
643 Smithfield Street
Pittsburgh, Pennsylvania 15222
U.S.A.
1-800-788-7654
Or visit our web site and on-line catalog at
www.dorrancepublishing.com.

Previous Literary Credits
Anthologies

1. *Golden Poems of the Western World*
   Title: *Christmas Morn*, Published by World of Poetry (1981)

2. *Our Twentieth Century's Greatest Poets*
   Title: *Brothers All*, Published by World of Poetry (1982)

3. *Twentieth Century Poets*
   Title: *Make A Better World*, Published by World of Poetry (1990)

4. *World Treasury of Golden Poetry*
   Title: *A World of Freedom*, Published by World of Poetry (1990)

5. *Outstanding Poets of 1994*
   Title: *What Does This Country Mean to Me*, Published by World of Poetry (1994)

Books

Speaking From the Heart
Year Published
1996
By Vantage Press, Inc.
New York, NY

Inducted into the International Poetry Hall of Fame (1997)
Hall of Fame Museum, World Wide Web
Location: http://www.poets.com/MertisJohn.html

A Special Thanks

A special thanks to Rosalind A. Wilson for her kind attention and her professionalism in helping me to get this manuscript typed. She worked with me in my office for countless hours.

Contents

Acknowledgments ix

Author's Note x

First and Foremost xi

A Part of Me xii

Chapter One 1

Chapter Two 4

Chapter Three 14

Chapter Four 19

Chapter Five 26

Chapter Six 29

Chapter Seven 34

Chapter Eight 38

Chapter Nine 45

Chapter Ten 51

Chapter Eleven 61

Chapter Twelve 70

Chapter Thirteen 82

Chapter Fourteen 116

Chapter Fifteen 133

Chapter Sixteen 137

Chapter Seventeen 153

Chapter Eighteen 158

Chapter Nineteen 164

Chapter Twenty 169

Chapter Twenty-one 173

Photo Credits 177

Index 182

Acknowledgments

First, I give thanks to Almighty God for bringing me forth and for giving me the knowledge and the dream to write this book. I also thank him for giving me the strength to complete it, because this book should have been completed some years ago. However, there was a period of time after the passing of my brother, Little Willie John, that I could not find the strength to continue writing this story. So I thank God for directing me to resume writing, after years of saying I could not.

I give thanks to my parents, Mertis and Lillie John. My completing this book is something they both wanted.

Also, I give thanks to my lovely and charming wife, Verlaine. She is my queen, as well as my wife. It took lots of love and understanding to stand by me while I labored for many, many hours to complete this book.

I want to also acknowledge and give my special thanks to my Creative Writing instructor, Dr. Steven Channault, at Wayne State University. Thank you for your instruction and inspiration! You played an integral part in my success as an author.

Further, I thank my sister, Mable, for her encouragement; my dear friend for so many years, Janie Bradford; and Claudette Robinson, formerly of *The Miracles*.

To my friend and right-hand man of many years, a musician and my A&R Director for Meda Records, Joseph E. Hunter.

All of you have been a tremendous help to me in various ways.

Author's Note

When I first began writing songs, way back in 1949 and 1950, I had no idea that I would some day write a book. Now I have written more than one! If I had known beforehand that I would write a book, I would have kept written records from the very beginning. I would have documented the times and events even further by photographing events to help maintain the memories.

My mother was good at keeping records, she wrote notes and saved clippings from newspapers and magazines. However, she was not always aware of all of the events which took place away from home, outside Detroit.

I wish I had kept better records, or possessed a greater memory. Since I did not, a lot of this book was written from memory. I apologize if I should have mentioned anyone in any instance in the book but failed to do so. I tried to remember and mention as many events as possible which have played a role in my life. I also tried to mention all who were involved, but I may have failed to remember all.

As I take my mind back to the years when my brothers and sisters were singing as a group, I wish it had been better documented. Inasmuch as it was not, I relied on my memory.

Inasmuch as all the above is true, at the same time, in writing this book I wanted the reader to see me as a writer. You have no doubt, read many autobiographies and I have also. However, I wanted this autobiography to stand alone in style, content, and information. But at the same time, I wanted it to be something that draws your attention to it, then holds you until you have finished reading the entire book.

As you read, hopefully you will be entertained, inspired, as well as informed.

First and Foremost

Recognition of God

Any man who fails to recognize the need for God in
Everything he attempts to do...
Isn't a man after all.

> Copyright 1996
> By Mertis John

A Part of Me

Music is a big part of my life
I was conceived in it—born in it,
And I will live all of my life in it.

I read it, I write it, I play it, I sing it,
I listen to it, I meditate with it,
And I very strongly—love it.

        Copyright 1996
        By Mertis John

Chapter One

This story begins to unfold in the city of Detroit as I write about myself, my life, my family, our upbringing, our experiences, and our careers.

We grew up on the east side of the city, first in an area called *Black Bottom*. This area was populated mostly by Blacks and Italians. Later, my family moved from this area to the northeast part of the city. But don't let me get ahead of myself. I'll get back to that later.

My family lived across the street from a trucking company warehouse, Associate Trucking. We were living at 2120 Monroe Street at that time. Many times the trucking company would have broken boxes of goods, such as candy and other things kids would like. They would call us over and give the broken boxes of candy or other goodies to us. On the next corner, there was our neighborhood grocery store where we were frequently sent to buy needed items. The streetcar line also ran on our street. It was the Baker Line. One other thing that's fresh in my memory about those times is the sight of the horse drawn wagon that brought us milk, butter, eggs, and juice. Each day those items were left on the front porch at the door. The man on the wagon would never stop until it was time to pay him and that was once a week. What amazed me most is that the horse was never told when to stop, but he knew each house when to stop and when to move on. Our school, Duffield Elementary, was a few short blocks away. It was the pride of the area, very large with three floors. Joe Louis, the Greatest Heavyweight Boxer in my time, had attended the same school some years earlier. I feel he was the greatest boxer ever.

I'm a member of a large family. There were six boys, three girls, father, and mother, a total of eleven. Allow me to introduce my family. I'd like to

Mertis John

start with my parents, they are Mertis and Lillie John. The children in order of age are: Mable, Mertis, Haywood, Mildred, William (later to be known to the world as "Little Willie John"), Delores, Ernest, Raymond, and Toronto. Willie's full name is William Edward John. The family didn't call him "William" or "Willie" until years later after he had his first record. The name William Edward came from our grandfather on my father's side. Also, it came from a friend who was probably my father's best friend at that time. We didn't call Raymond "Raymond" either until years later, after he became a singer. His full name is Raymond Nathaniel John. I don't recall why Mother Dear named him Raymond, but I do remember a close friend of the family by the name of Nathaniel. Nathaniel asked mother to give him his name, which she did. We were taught to call our mother "Mother Dear". Even Daddy called her Mother Dear so that we would too. We called our father "Daddy" and most of the time Mother Dear did also.

Now at this time Mable, myself, Haywood, and Mildred were all attending Duffield Elementary School in our neighborhood. All of us were doing well in school and we were always chosen to be members of the school choir. Sometimes we would sing alone, just our family group. Also, we were given roles in the school plays. They did this because they knew our parents had us singing together as a group in my mother's church and in the community. A little later, Edward would be enrolled into school at age five. Now five of us were attending Duffield Elementary School. Despite his young age, Edward had been singing two years and wanted to be added to the family's singing group. We were taught by our parents that school was a very essential learning vehicle for life and that we must go to school and learn to make something worthwhile of ourselves.

They especially wanted us to become entertainers, musicians, or teachers. Even a preacher would have been fine with Mother Dear. So they started exposing us to singing, acting, playing musical instruments, etc. Daddy played the guitar, harmonica, and Jew's harp. He taught me to play the harmonica and Jew's when I was about seven or eight. Mother Dear would sing. They asked us to study hard and obey the teachers. Now Edward's first day in school was approaching and after being told to obey and to avoid trouble just as all of us before him had been taught, he encountered trouble the very first day of school. His teacher asked him to do something that he didn't want to do. He told her that he didn't have to do it. "Further, if you mess with me, I'll put my big brother on you," he stated. I was the big brother that he was talking about at the time. I had no knowledge of what had transpired in the classroom or between he and the teacher. Even if I had, I would have never upheld him. What he had said frightened the teacher so much that she shut him up in the classroom closet and she called my father to come and get him. This made Daddy furious to know Willie had disobeyed both him and the teacher. He rushed to the school not in his son's defense, but to console the teacher. He assured

My Life and Experiences in the Entertainment World

the teacher that she had nothing to fear from him or me. He then told Edward he had a special lesson to teach him. After getting home, Daddy gave him a lesson never to be forgotten. "Always obey the teachers. I'm sending you to school to learn," he said. Of course, a whipping followed, an unforgettable one. After that we didn't have to worry about Edward getting into trouble for a long time.

At the age of three, everyone around Edward knew that he would be a great entertainer in conversation. He would hold manly conversations at that early age. He inquired about everything around him and also about things he thought of. He also had a very special interest in women at that early age. They fascinated him, even to the touch. That disturbed Mother Dear. When someone would come to the door of our home, he would open it and greet them as well as any adult would do. We were all taught to do this.

In June of 1943, before summer vacation was to start, we went to school one Monday morning as usual. When we arrived we noticed that the usual school atmosphere did not exist. Things were in disarray. White students and Black students were fighting each other. We didn't understand why at first, then we heard the news.

The day before, which was Sunday, it was said that a White man had thrown a Black mother's baby over the Belle Isle bridge to his death. We were unaware of this. However, it was clear that there would be no school. Parents who had sent their children to school that morning were coming to pick them up. We were going back home, too. As we passed through the doors and got outside, we saw Mother Dear coming to get us. We heard her yelling, "Come on, I'm taking you back home."

On the way home she explained to us that a race riot had begun the evening before. She heard the news after we had left for school. The riot lasted for several days. Police cars, street cars, and private cars were turned over and burned. Also there were street fights between adults. A number of people were hurt and there were some fatal casualties as well. The National Guard was called in to quell the disturbance. None of my family was hurt.

Chapter Two

Mother Dear and Daddy gave us some good news! We were moving to another house, a better house in another neighborhood. We were anxious to move, meet new friends, and transfer to new schools. We moved to the Davison and Dequindre area where the Washington Elementary and Cleveland Junior High Schools are located. Our new address was 14503 Dequindre. I became a Safety Patrol Squad Member while at Washington School. My grades were an average of B+ which they liked, so I was given a very important post on the squad. It happened to be at the corner of Davison and Dequindre, a very busy intersection in the city then, and it still is. A Detroit police officer was always on duty with us at that post. They accepted nothing but the best from those of us on that very important post. They got the best from us, too. If they had not, we would have been removed from that post immediately.

At Washington School we met new friends. We also met Ms. Laura K. Pickins, the vocal music teacher, who was later to become our first manager. She fell in love with us, and we in turn fell in love with her. It became a mutual admiration. Delores, the youngest sister, was enrolled into school about this time. By the way, we called her "Gaynell," her middle name. Ms. Pickins kept the family busy in school while Mother Dear and Daddy kept us busy at home, singing at one event after another. Ms. Pickins was impressed more than just mildly by the family's singing. She was so impressed that she contacted our parents by phone asking if she could come to the home to meet them. She was told to feel free to come to the home, that they also would like to meet her. When she came to our home, she made a huge impression on my parents.

My Life and Experiences in the Entertainment World

She began to tell them how she loved our singing. Then she went on to say that we should pursue a career in singing, and that someone who was familiar with the business should be acquired to direct the career. As the conversation continued, my parents became more impressed with this person who was so concerned about the singing career of their children. That took a lot for my father, he was not easily impressed by anyone, especially when his family was involved. As the conversation went on she told them of outlets she knew of and mentioned people that she could talk with who would get more exposure for the group. Being a teacher from a well educated and respected family, she knew a lot of influential people. There were several ministers in her family, the Campbell Family, who ministered to large congregations. Her grandfather was the pastor of the Russell Street Baptist Church. And she knew of other large churches where the ministers and congregations would be glad to have us come and sing at their churches. We were allowed to sing only Gospel and Patriotic songs at that time.

My parents agreed to allow her to begin guiding our singing career. They had gained a lot of confidence in her. We began to rehearse new songs. Whenever we rehearsed and the weather was warm, the windows and doors of our home were open. We attracted an audience during each practice without leaving home. As we sang, first the porch would become crowded, then the yard, and before we knew it, the house was surrounded with people from our neighborhood. As we would end a song, we would hear hand clapping and other sounds. We were unaware that they were there listening until we would hear the clapping and voices.

When we were not singing together, Edward (Willie) was usually singing somewhere for someone, or maybe for several people. He would sing for anyone who would listen to him. People would ask him to sing wherever he would go. Many times when we expected him to be home, he was not there. We would have to go looking for him. We would find him in the middle of a crowd, the smallest person there, holding an audience. We would have to take him home and explain to Mother Dear where he was, and that he was in no trouble. He was only doing what he loved doing most...performing. At other times, the people who asked him to sing would bring him home to let Mother Dear know that he was fine, and that they had detained Edward so that he could sing for them.

Time and time again, he would come home with money and other little gifts. He would have to return the gifts because Mother Dear thought he had asked for them. We could not bring anything home without our parent's permission. Edward would say to her, "Well you like for me to sing. They asked me to sing, so I did and they gave me these gifts." Mother would then talk with the people and after doing so, being assured this was true, she would be satisfied and allowed him to keep what had been given to him. She was proud however, to know that so many people enjoyed her son's singing. She would even tell her friends about such

Mertis John

incidents, especially Mrs. Stubbs. She was the mother of Levi Stubbs, the leader of the Four Tops' fame singing group.

In the meantime, our manager, Ms. Pickins, was lining up dates for us. She was successful in getting a date at the famed Book Cadillac Hotel in Detroit (later named "The Sheraton Hotel"). This was certainly a performance to be cherished for life, especially because we were told that Black people were not allowed to perform at that hotel. We didn't know anything about that, we were too young. The performance was a total success! Our parents were very pleased with this appearance. The audience was very warm and they were thoroughly receptive.

Our next performance was at our manager's grandfather's church, The Russell Street Baptist Church. On the following Sunday, Ms. Pickins came to our home to drive us to the church. We were ready to leave but Daddy stayed home. We said our goodbyes, then Daddy gave his usual instructions to us. It was always the same, "Sing good." Mother Dear would always say, "Remember, make me proud." He then told Ms. Pickins to take good care of his children, then we were off.

When it was time for us to sing, we really got into it. We must have given them a good performance because they really responded to our singing in a very favorable way. They began to do something we had not experienced before. Even before we finished singing, they began to throw money on the floor all around us. This inspired us to sing more, and we sang the best that we could. They were very pleased with our singing. We were equally pleased because they had accepted us, and our talent, in a big way. Aside from the money that they had thrown on the floor, an offering, which was usually all we would get, was also collected for us. Needless to say, this was by far the largest amount of money that we had received for our work up to that time. In addition to the money that had been collected, Willie was given money by Reverend Campbell, just for himself, to go purchase a suit, shirt, tie, and shoes. That's right—a complete outfit for Willie! We were invited to come back and sing again.

As you would expect, we were all very happy; the church, Reverend Campbell, our parents, and us too. Daddy could hardly wait to see us walk through the door. The first thing he asked Ms. Pickins as we came in the house was, "How did they do?" That was always his first question when he had not been with us.

She was smiling from ear to ear, as she replied, "Very good."

Then Daddy asked, "How much money did we make?"

"It was very good. I haven't had a chance to count it all yet. I had most of it under my car seat, and the rest of it in my purse."

Then Daddy said, "Come on let's count it."

After the money had been counted, Daddy gave Ms. Pickins her share. I'm not really sure how much money was collected for us that day, but it must have been between six and seven hundred dollars. Daddy offered his usual celebration that he would do after every successful

My Life and Experiences in the Entertainment World

performance. He treated us to all the cake, ice cream, pop, and potato chips that we wanted.

The next engagement we had was at one of the largest Black Methodist churches in the city. I believe it was located on Brush Street. Here, it was a repeat of what we had experienced at the Russell Street Baptist Church a few days prior. The reception was just as warm and the collection that they gave us was about the same.

Sometime later, our manager thought it would be a good idea for us to witness a performance by a young performer, since we were all young children ourselves. The most successful child performer at that time was a star who's home was in Detroit. He was none other than Sugar Child Robinson. He was about seven or eight years old at the time. He was a singer who also played the piano. In his act, he always got around to playing the piano with his elbows and fists, as well as with his fingers. He was a very pint-sized fellow. His age and unusual playing style had made him an instant hit. He was traveling all over the world playing to sold out audiences and now he was coming home. Yes, he was coming home and we would see him! He would be appearing at the famous Michigan Theater downtown. Lots of stage shows would come to the Michigan Theater then, but most all the acts and performers were White artists. The opening act on this show was a White singer whose name was Kitty Kallen. Most all Black artists played at other places in the city at that time. Sugar Child could hear a song just once, then go to the piano and play it from memory. One of the songs he would perform then was "Caldonia, Caldonia" another was the "Sugar Child Boogie Woogie."

Our manger took us to see him and we thoroughly enjoyed his performance. After the show, we were allowed to meet Sugar Child. What a thrill! We hoped that someday we would be just as successful as he, singing to large audiences all over the world.

When we returned home, we were excited to let Mother Dear and Daddy know how much we had enjoyed him. They told us that we would be able to do the same thing. Many years later after ending his career, Sugar Child was working as an account executive for Radio Station WGPR in Detroit. I would visit the station to meet with the program director, Joe Spencer, to schedule my records air time at that station. I had formed my own record company, Meda Records, at that time. Sugar Child and I would talk about the business as it had been in the years past. I also owned a barber shop not far from the radio station and I invited Sugar Child to come by. He accepted, and I cut his hair on several occasions. We talked about the business each time he would come in.

Willie, along with our other brothers and sisters, continued to sing at home every week; on Sundays in our mother's church, The Triumph Church; in school; and at community affairs. A while later, people in several churches remembered how they had enjoyed the John's singing so much that they would ask Mother Dear to bring us to their church to sing

Mertis John

for them. This she did after many requests. This took us all over the city. We were first known as "The John Family." Later, we became "The United Five."

At this time, Willie was getting better with his high tenor voice which sometimes sounded like soprano. So Mother Dear told him to start singing some solos. He did and enjoyed it because this focused more attention on him. He always liked to have everyone's attention and hold it. This he did very well.

During the time we were singing in the various churches, Mable and I were taught Bible stories by Mother Dear. We had to learn them verbatim and recite them at various church programs. Sometimes I had to ask Mable questions, and she would supply the answers. I remember the first story that I had to learn and do without Mable. It was the story of Hannah, who was barren but she wanted a son so very much. She began to pray to God daily for a son:

I Samuel 1:10
And she was in bitterness of soul, and prayed unto the Lord, and wept sore.

I Samuel 1:11
And she vowed a vow, and said, O Lord of Hosts, if thou wilt indeed look on the affliction of thine handmaid, and remember me, and not forget thine handmaid, but wilt give unto thine handmaid a man child, then I will give him unto the Lord, all the days of his life, and there shall no razor come upon his head.

I Samuel 1:12–13
And it came to pass, as she continued praying before the Lord, that Eli marked her mouth. Now Hannah, she spake in her heart; only her lips moved, but her voice was not heard: Therefore, Eli thought she had been drunken. (When Hannah let him know that she had nothing to drink, but was only sorry that she had no son, he answers her thus).

I Samuel 1:17
Then Eli answered and said, go in peace: And the God of Israel grant thee thy petition that thou has asked of him.

I Samuel 1:20
Wherefore it came to pass, when the time was come about after Hannah had conceived, that she bare a son, and called his name Samuel, saying because I have asked him of the Lord.

Mother Dear told me that after I was conceived, she had also asked God for a son because she had none at that time. I believe that is why she taught this story to me when I was a very young child. After my birth, she

My Life and Experiences in the Entertainment World

was puzzled as to what she should name me. After pondering for a good while, she finally named me after my father, "Mertis." I'm glad that she did. It's odd and it fits with my personality.

Willie Auditions for Talent Show

Willie auditioned for a talent show at the Times Square Theater here in Detroit. He went on the show and came home with first prize with the family trio. This made him very enthusiastic about show business.

This eventually took him to the once famous Paradise Theater, now known as Orchestra Hall. This was *the* number one place for Black entertainers to perform on stage in Detroit. Each Friday a new show would come to town to play the famous Paradise. I still remember the address of the theater, 3711 Woodward Avenue. The building still remains, but shows have long since changed. In those days, it brought in entertainers with such big names as Count Basie, Duke Ellington, Sarah Vaughn, Louis Jordan, Josephine Baker, Dinah Washington, Peg Leg Bates, Ella Fitzgerald, Billie Holiday, Buddy Johnson, Billy Eskstien, Nat Cole, and the list goes on and on.

Now it was about time for Willie to go on that same stage, but as an amateur in a contest. Well, he did go on, and he won first prize—not only that week, but for the next two Thursdays to follow! He received a $75.00 gold watch each week for three consecutive weeks. At the end of the third week, he was told he could not compete again because he was winning too many times. His status was now that of a professional.

Later, he entered an amateur contest to determine the State Champion Classic Singer, and the results were the same as before. He won five consecutive years. He now dreamed of a serious career. He wanted to be more than just a singer, he wanted to be the best.

A Word About Daddy

Now Daddy loved music and sports; such as baseball, boxing, and wrestling. He loved seeing his children displaying their talents. He taught us to stick together and help each other to be successful in whatever we would set out to do. He also had hobbies, fishing and hunting. He kept about eight reels and rods in good working condition for fishing. Aside from his own use, he made sure he had some for family members' use in case any of us went along with him on fishing trips. He would always encourage us to go along with him, but only occasionally would we go. I went with him a few times but I never loved it nearly as much as he did. He really wanted to teach me to fish as well as he, but I really didn't have that much interest in it. He would leave many times early in the morning and would not return until the following evening late.

As for hunting, he would only hunt small game; squirrels, rabbits, and pheasant. Any time he was off from his work, depending on the time of year, he would either go fishing or hunting. On many occasions I saw him bring home five or six squirrels or rabbits. When he would go fishing he

Mertis John

would bring back enough for the whole family, he knew his hobbies well. He also wanted to teach me to hunt but I'm not good at that either.

One day, when we were still young, Daddy loaded the first five of us siblings; Mable, myself, Haywood, Mildred, and Willie, along with Mother Dear into the car. He drove all of us downtown until he got to the county jail. He then stopped the car and pointed to the building. He said, "I'll tell you, it's the jail. That's the place they bring you when you do bad things. So don't you ever do anything that's bad." Then he said, "Take a look at the windows, you see they all have bars on them. If you're locked up you cannot get out, and it's a bad place to be."

Willie was the only one of us who felt that he could get out of jail. After Daddy finished talking to us about the jail, Willie said, "They can't keep me in that jail. If they lock me up in there I will get out." That's the way Willie was, thinking that he could come up with a solution for any situation. He was absolutely confident that he could.

Now getting back to Daddy, he went to that much effort to show that he wanted us to always stay out of trouble with the law and the consequences if we did not. Well, that lesson did have an impact on my life. I always remembered seeing those bars on the windows of the jail. I knew then that I never wanted to be on the other side of those bars. It taught me that I had to carry myself in such a way that I would never have to be incarcerated. On the other hand, as I grew up, I learned that you can find yourself on the other side of those bars without having done wrong. It's happened countless times, Martin Luther King Jr. and many others. However, I feel if I had to, that I would be capable of bringing facts to light so that I would be proven innocent and consequently exonerated.

I never knew my father's parents. His mother's name was Morning John. She passed away when he was only sixteen years old. His father, Bill John, passed away before any of Daddy's children would have a chance to get to know him. My father talked quite a bit to us about his parents. We know that he loved them both very much.

Mother Dear

By this point in the book, I'm sure you know that my parents had and raised nine children. As a young child, one has no perception of how to rate their parents as for how good they are. It was the same with me when I was very young. Even though I could see how they treated me and my siblings, I was not capable of rating them as good or bad. Most all young children feel that their parents are the best, even when they are not.

As I grew up and became a young man I could look back and see where I came from. I then became qualified to rate and/or evaluate my parents. I knew then that they had been good parents for us.

As I look back on my life from my very earliest remembrance, I can see that Mother Dear was very loving and caring. She was also very detailed in the things that she did. It was a joy for her to take care of all of us, to feed

My Life and Experiences in the Entertainment World

us, cook for us, to keep us clean, to teach us, and to keep the house clean. Aside from that, she did her best to keep the nine of us happy and to keep Daddy happy too.

She always had time in her busy schedule to sit down and read to us. She would also teach us poetry that she wanted us to recite. One of the first books she introduced and would read to us, was the Holy Bible. She would sing songs to us for our pleasure and she would also teach songs to us to learn to sing for her pleasure, and the pleasure of many others in the church. One of the first songs that she sang to me was, "In the Garden." I shall always remember it.

Yes, I can truthfully say that Mother Dear has always been a good mother. Not because she's my mother, but because the facts prove that she is. In addition to what I have already said about her, she also counseled us about whatever needed to be learned. She always wanted to do what was right in every situation. She made sure that we knew right from wrong.

I remember a time when we were very young and the house next door to us caught fire at night. We were all asleep. We didn't always just wake up when she first called us to get up. However, on this occasion, she came to our room just once, snapping her fingers and at the same time shouting to us, "Get up, get up, the house next door is on fire. Come on with me now. I'm getting you out of the house."

We all got up at that initial call to us. There was no hesitation at all. She got us all out safe and sound. By the way, our house suffered very little damage, only the exterior was slightly scorched. I remember that night very well, and I have also heard Mother Dear recount it to us many times.

Many times I have seen her cook for people whom she didn't know. Our family is large but I have seen it swell when others were taken in. She taught us early, this verse from the Bible, Exodus 20:12. It says, "Honor thy father and thy mother that thy days may be long upon the land which the Lord thou God giveth thee." Also, the same reading is found in Deuteronomy 5:16 and in Ephesians 6:1–3. I know how Mother Dear felt about her parents, and I do know that she did honor them both while they were alive. I truly feel that God has given her longevity because of that fact. She is now ninety years old. The oldest of her siblings, my Uncle Jessie (her brother), lived to become three months short of his ninetieth birthday.

Proverbs 12:4 says, "A virtuous woman is a crown to her husband." That's what Daddy had in my Mother Dear, "a virtuous woman." I'm happy that the time eventually came when I could evaluate my parents in an honest and truthful way. That's why I feel honored to talk about my mother here. I'm very proud of the fact that she is my mother. No one has any more integrity than she. She has been a genuine mother right from the very beginning. She needs all the honor that I can give to her. I'm proud of the fact that I do.

My mother's parents were Eddie and Rebecca Robinson. Some of my siblings and I had the opportunity to meet both of them when we traveled

Mertis John

down to their home when we were very young. The occasion was to see as many of our relatives as possible when we were in the New Orleans vicinity. My grandmother visited us in Detroit on several occasions. She is the grandparent that I came to know best.

I'm displaying a photograph of her in this book. It is photo number five.

Mother Dear told us often about how her mother would whip her and her siblings when they would do wrong. We asked Mother Dear, because we wanted to know if she whipped them like Mother Dear whipped us. I asked my grandmother when I got the chance if she whipped them. She told me, "Yes, and I will whip you now if you ever need one." All the time as she spoke, she kept a little smile on her face. But I had heard Mother Dear and Uncle Jessie say many times that she was a firm disciplinarian. When I was young she would say to me, "You can come visit me if you obey, but if you don't obey I will certainly whip you."

A Promise Mother Dear Kept

When my brothers and sisters and I were teenagers, my mother would tell us how she wanted to travel. She couldn't at that time and the reason was obvious. She and Daddy were bringing up nine children which were first and foremost in their lives, and there was no way in the world that she would shirk her responsibility to the family. They would leave the responsibility of our care to no one else. What she planned was to bring the nine of us up properly and then we would be able to take care of ourselves. After that, she planned to do extensive traveling. Willie would tell her many times that someday he would send her every place that she wanted to go. He was dreaming then of the success he would some day have and that he would be able to send her anywhere she desired to go.

During the years we were growing up and she dreamed of traveling, there was really no money in the family for her to experience that dream. Daddy was working at an automobile factory and taking care of the family. Not much money for traveling could come from a salary that the auto plants paid. So Mother Dear really didn't know for certain how her dream would become a reality. She did, however, feel that her sons would contribute to the cost of her traveling. I heard her mention that possibility on occasions.

As time passed and Willie was signed and sealed to a recording contract and turning out hit records, Mother would travel to some of the cities where he would be performing. At that, she was beginning to realize her wish to travel. She came to meet and know a number of entertainers, musicians, and others who were in the entertainment industry. Willie would also send her to other places.

In later years, after Willie's passing, when Mable had joined the Ray Charles aggregation to lead his singing group, "The Raylettes," she moved to California to be where the Ray Charles base is located. Mother Dear would then spend the summer months at home in Detroit and the winter

My Life and Experiences in the Entertainment World

months in California at Mable's home. When Mable would go on vacations, she would take mother wherever in the world she would go. Mother would also travel to various locations to witness and enjoy the shows. She was able to travel as she had dreamed she would do. This lasted for more than thirty years. She loved flying here, there, and everywhere - all over the world. This continued until she became ill.

In 1991, Mother Dear suffered a stroke which limited her activities. She had, up to that point, been very active all her life. The following year she suffered a second stroke after which the doctor said he didn't want her to try walking. Due to her condition, she has not been able to travel since. Mable then took over keeping her and saw that she had the best of care. We can't go to her home in Detroit and expect to hear her say, "Come on in. What took you so long?" any longer. However, I do enjoy talking to her on the phone and hearing her loving voice say, "Hi, Mert. I love you." I also enjoy traveling to California to visit her and sitting with her each day that I'm there.

I am so thankful Mother Dear that you were able to travel just as you told us that you would do, way back when.

Chapter Three

We were all in school now. Mable and I both were in junior high, attending Cleveland Junior High School. Ernest, Raymond, and Toronto (in that order) were the last to enter school. They, along with Haywood, Mildred, Willie, and Delores were still attending Washington Elementary School.

At this point, Ms. Pickings saw so much growth and experience in the family that she felt she should no longer manage our singing affairs. She decided to retire from these management duties. So we no longer had our first manager. However, we always maintained our love and respect for each other.

Back in elementary school, I had started to play the violin. I tried very hard to learn to play it, but after a while I was convinced that this instrument was not for me. I really wanted to try the trumpet at that time. Again, just as I had done in elementary school, I signed up for the music class. Mr. Victor King was the instrumental music teacher at Cleveland Junior High. I must say too, that he was a good teacher. When he asked me what instrument I played, I told him I wanted to play the trumpet. He looked at me and then said, "Son, you can't play the trumpet. You're going to play the trombone." Then he handed me one and said, "This trombone is what you're going to play." So that was my introduction to the trombone. At that, I gravitated to the trombone. I played it through Junior High and High School, and continued playing it except for the time when I was in the military service, sometime later.

Even though music was my family's number one love and career goal, that was not all we did. Both Mother Dear and Daddy were firm believers that we should have a well rounded knowledge in all phases of life. By this

My Life and Experiences in the Entertainment World

time the oldest children were taught to keep the house clean. They washed walls and windows, mopped the floors and waxed them and cleaned the kitchen. The girls learned to cook, wash, and iron. In addition to this, the boys had to keep the furnace clean and make fires for heat, take out the ashes, and bring in the coal for heat. We all had chores to perform and we had to do them well. That was an absolute must.

When the boys weren't doing chores at home, we were selling newspapers. I had a *Detroit News* route and also shined shoes. In the winter we shoveled people's snowy walkways or whatever else we could find to do.

At age twelve, I became a Boy Scout. In my neighborhood our Scout Master at that time was canvassing the area for new boys who he believed would be good potential scouts. Mr. Woods was the scout master's name. He talked to me about the scouts and asked me if I would like to become a member. I told him I thought that I would. He subsequently spoke with my mother and father about it and they permitted me to join the troop. I became a member of Troop Number 518. Then I began to study what being a scout meant. I also learned the way I was supposed to carry myself. But those things were no different from what I had already been taught by my parents. The only new information that I learned was how to live and survive in the woods, etc. and how to tie different knots for various uses.

I remember the first field trip that I was a part of. We left during the day and we were driven to Holly, Michigan to camp out. We were to spend the remainder of the day, all that night, and to break camp the next day and arrive home at 6:00 P.M. My parents got confused with the time I was to return home. When we did return, they had been looking and waiting for me for hours. I'll never forget the look on their faces when they met me. Daddy didn't want me to go camping again.

I have always been an inquisitive person and this made me ask many questions. Subsequently, I enjoyed reading and researching things of interest to me. I became an avid reader of history because history interested me most. Not so much American History, but World History was a prominent interest of mine. With American History, for me, there always seemed to be something missing. I couldn't figure out what it was at that time, but as I continued to read and research, I found that American History had shortchanged the Black people. The facts of Black History were omitted from the books we were reading in school. When I was very young, I remember asking my mother about the bombing of Pearl Harbor, the act which put the United States into World War II. I asked her where Pearl Harbor was located. She said she wasn't sure but said she thought it was not far from New York City. I said, "Oh that's not too far from us!" I later found it on the world map and I always remembered where it was located. Years later, I was fortunate enough to visit there on several occasions. That history is embedded in my memory forever. It took my mind back to the morning our neighbor, Mr. Calvin Gooden, was holding a newspaper as it partially rested on the fence that separated our two houses. He and my dad were

Mertis John

reading about the attack the Japanese had made on the United States Navy at Pearl Harbor on that regretful Sunday morning, December 7, 1941.

Later, after getting out of school for the summer, I found a job at a car wash, which we called a "wash rack," located on Livernois and Puritan. It was one of the best in the city. We would wash and simonize cars. I had just turned thirteen years of age. We would wash cars seven days a week, working from 8:00 A.M. to 6:00 P.M. On Sundays we would work from 8:00 A.M. to 3:00 P.M. When my family was singing on Sundays, I was allowed to leave a little early in order to go home and get ready. I was able to leave early only the times that it was necessary to do so. Not only did we wash cars, we also would simonize and blue coral cars which would give them a finish that made them look like new.

At that time that area of Livernois was populated with many used car lots. My boss was Dave Ford. Dave had a contract with most of the used car dealers in that area whereby we were to keep the cars clean, simonized, and looking good for the potential buyers. This kept us busy all of the time, rain or shine, warm or cold.

When I was hired, I had been told by someone that I could get a job there and sure enough I was hired immediately. After I had worked there for a while, I asked my boss if I could bring my next oldest brother, Haywood, to work there too. He said I could. The next day when I went to work I took Haywood with me. Dave hired him that day. My brother Haywood and I worked there together for years. I stayed there until I was eighteen.

After I had worked at the wash rack for the summer and it was time to end the summer vacation, I prepared to return to school. Then Dave told me that if I could get there early enough after school, he wanted me to continue working every day. I went to school, registered and got my schedule of classes and hours. After school, I went to the bus stop as fast as I could and boarded the Davison shuttle bus. I was at the job in time to work three hours after school. Then Dave told me to continue coming each day after school, and at the regular time on weekends, 8:00 A.M.

At that time, I saw I had a regular job to keep. Also, the pay began to increase a little. That made me feel extremely happy about myself. I had been hoping that I could find a job that would be long lasting as well as profitable, at least until I graduated from high school. Here I had found it.

Eventually, I suppose when I was fifteen or sixteen years old, Mr. Ford added another duty to my routine. He allowed me to drive cars from the used car lots to the wash rack for washing or simonizing. That gave me an additional thrill for working there! I had already been allowed to drive cars that were inside the building or on the property. Believe it or not, Mr. Ford couldn't drive.

One day after I picked up a car, I did something very stupid. As I was driving back to the wash rack, something wild came over me. All at once, I said to myself, "I'll see how fast this car will go." I pressed the accelerator down and I got up to seventy miles an hour. There I was on a city street

My Life and Experiences in the Entertainment World

driving seventy miles an hour in a residential area with no license. Then I began to think, "You fool, slow this car down!" I immediately slowed down to twenty miles an hour. I then said to myself that I would never be so stupid again. I could have killed or injured myself or others. I began to thank God for taking care of me and for not allowing me to hurt anyone, nor any property. When I returned to the wash rack, Mr. Ford could sense that I had done something wrong. The engine was hotter than it should have been for driving the distance I had driven. He looked around the car and everything looked fine. Then he asked me if everything was all right. I told him yes, and he never said another word about it to me again.

There was another silly thing that I had done previously and I learned a lesson from. This had happened much earlier in life when I was about five years old. One day, my father had just given me some coins, of which at least one was a penny. As always after getting money, I was very happy. I began to play with the coins as a child often does. In doing so, I put the penny up to my mouth. The penny fell into my mouth. My father had turned away from me and he was talking to Mother Dear. I tried to bring it back but I couldn't. I choked and my parents ran to me. Daddy began to beat me on the back. However, the penny did not return. They then put me in the car and drove to the doctor's office. However, the doctor was not in. Outside the doctor's office Daddy began to beat on my back again. To the relief of all, the penny fell onto the sidewalk. Mother Dear and Daddy let out a shout, we were all happy and we returned home. I was told never to put money up to my mouth again. I really didn't need to be told, because that experience was a lesson within itself. I have never forgotten that incident and I never did anything like that again.

Now Back to the Wash Rack:
My father was employed at the Dodge Main Automobile Factory long before I went to work at the wash rack. However, for some reason, he was laid off for a short while during the time I was working at the wash rack. At the time of this layoff, he asked me if I could get him a job where I was working. I told him I would ask if he could come. When I asked Dave if he could come his answer was yes. So Daddy went with Haywood and me the next day and began to wash cars with the rest of us who were there. He worked with us for a short period of time until he was called back to his regular job at Dodge Main. There in the basement of the wash rack is where we would change into work clothes, rubber pants and tops. Also, rubber boots were worn. At the end of the day we would change back into street clothes. Now that wasn't the only thing that the basement was used for.

At the end of the day, many times there would be dice games in the basement. When Daddy was there he would join in the games. I never touched the dice. I didn't want to because of Mother Dear's dislike for gambling. She had taught us never to gamble. However, I would watch and bet on the side. Mother Dear had taught us that gambling was wrong. It was sinful. But we knew Daddy sometimes got into games.

That first day after work for Daddy, he joined in the game. I did as I had always done and had my bets on the side. Even though Daddy knew exactly what I was doing, he didn't say a word or try and stop me. Even after leaving and on the way home, he said nothing about it. We talked as usual all the way home. He never said anything to me about it. Instead, as soon as we got into the house he went to Mother Dear and said, "Mother, guess what your son has been doing? Gambling."

She then came over to me and shouted to me, "Boy I had better never again hear of you trying to gamble. Do you understand me?"

I, in my frightened state answered, "Yes ma'am." I was so ashamed I was already whipped even without getting any physical blows. Daddy just stood back looking and laughing. I didn't have to be told again. From that moment on, I promised Mother Dear, and then God, that I would never have anything to do with dice again. I have always kept, and I shall continue to keep, that promise.

Along about that same time, I began to establish credit for myself. The first thing I did to acquire credit was to buy a watch for myself. There was a jewelry store on the same street where I worked. I went there to buy my first classy watch. I paid for it on a time basis. I wore it for dress only on Sundays and other occasions that were special. Then I began to buy pieces of furniture and all of my clothing. I paid all of the rent for the home where my family and I were living. I was, at that point, taking care of myself and have continued to do so since. That's the time I became an independent man. It was so easy for me to establish credit. Maybe since I had my father's name. Also, I knew where he was employed and his department number, as well as his badge number. When I was asked where I worked, I would never tell them I worked at the wash rack. Instead, I would tell them I worked at Dodge Main in Daddy's department and I would give them his badge number. Why they never questioned me, I really don't know. Daddy would have backed me up had it come to that. But I'm happy it turned out as it did. I never had any problem getting approved for credit. I paid all my bills on time, and have maintained a good credit rating.

When I decided to buy my first new car I was eighteen years old, just a minor in those days. Consequently, I had to have my dad co-sign for it. He gladly did. That is the only item which I needed a co-signer on. Daddy didn't have to pay one single note. He knew he wouldn't have to. I didn't have to borrow from any individual at any time to pay. By the way, borrowing is something I have always abstained from. I have always hated to do it, so I made sure that I wouldn't have to.

Chapter Four

The Things We Did As Children
As children, we did various things aside from our singing and going to church. All the boys loved sports just as Daddy did. We loved riding our bicycles, going to the parks, and going to the movies, etc. I bought myself a bicycle and I would ride it every chance I got. I would ride to the store and around the neighborhood. Sometimes Daddy wouldn't let me ride unless I took my brothers and sisters, so I was sure to ride them too. At the same time, Willie was also running the streets and as often as he could, hustling barber shops and on the streets. His prime streets were Davison, Hastings, Woodward, and John R. On the streets, he would sing and shine shoes. In the barber shops, he would shine shoes and run errands for the barbers and the patrons. When he was shining shoes, he would not hesitate to let them know that he could sing for them too. Now that was his favorite thing and he always ended by singing for them.

At other times Willie would go to the very popular Joe's Record Shop on Hastings Street. Joe Von Battles was the owner of the shop. He had all of the latest records that the Black community wanted. So Willie would go there and check them out. Joe had something else that attracted Willie. In the back there was a small recording studio and Willie learned all he could about how it worked.

When we wanted to see the young bad guys of boxing who were coming up, we would go to the Brewster Recreation Center which was nearby to watch them train.

A very popular park for Detroiters is located on the east side and right on the Detroit River. It's our famous Belle Isle. You can drive across the bridge over the Detroit River to gain access to the Isle, or you can cross the river by boat. Those are the only two ways to get across to the Island.

We would to go the Isle for picnics. We would also visit the zoo that's there. There are horses to ride and buggies pulled by ponies. Canoes are also available and we would take canoe rides, too. There are several baseball diamonds on the Island run by the City's Parks and Recreation Department. A lot of baseball is played there. For food, you find hot dogs, ice cram, potato chips, candy, and other treats are sold on the Island. However, that's not the most popular happening on the Island. There's golfing and there is also a beach where we would go to swim in the Detroit River. Still, I have not mentioned the most popular activity of all. The many cookouts that take place all over the Island when the weather is pleasant is the most popular activity. During the summer months, many people spend the night on the Island. It is necessary to get there very early to ensure getting a choice spot.

The Island also has a band shell. During the summer months, concerts are a big attraction on the Island too. Another thing the family would do is catch every good stage show that came to town. The most popular place was the Paradise Theatre. When we wanted to catch some thrill rides around a carnival atmosphere, we would go to the Eastwood Amusement Park and later Edgewater Park on West Seven Mile and Telegraph.

All of the boys played baseball and we kept up with what was happening on the major league baseball diamonds each day. We simply loved it. Some of the family would say that Ernest loved playing baseball more than he loved to eat. Believe me, we all loved to play the game of baseball. I would go to Tiger Stadium (it was Briggs Stadium then) and watch the games every chance I would get. I just loved seeing the teams play. Later, I tried out for the team that was sponsored by the Lasky Furniture Company, the Lasky Giants. I played left field. There were other fellows who played on my team and on teams we played against, who were very good and went on to play in the Major Leagues. Lennie Green whom I lived near and grew up with, started with the Lumpkin Cubs, a team we played against. He played several positions, including pitching, first base, and the outfield. Willie Kirkland played the outfield. He would hit balls farther than anyone that I saw play the game. We had a very good catcher, his name was Lonnie Smith. Joe Reed, our best pitcher, was a very good player too.

We had our own ball park called Dequindre Park. We also had our own bus for transportation. Our manager was Mr. Leroy Dozier. After Jackie Robinson completed his first season with the Brooklyn Dodgers in 1947, he traveled over the country playing with different ball clubs. He came to Detroit and played as a member of the Detroit Stars. He played at several positions that day. The game was played in our ball park. It was also the park of the Detroit Stars.

Lennie Green and Willie Kirkland played their way to the Major Leagues. Lennie played in the Major Leagues for twelve years playing for

My Life and Experiences in the Entertainment World

the Washington Senators, Baltimore Orioles and finally getting to play for his home team, the Detroit Tigers. In the Major Leagues, he was an outfielder. Willie Kirkland played for the San Francisco Giants after the team had moved from New York. He played along side of the great Willie Mays. As I was traveling on the road in show business, they were traveling with their ball clubs. We sometimes saw each other often. We would stay at the same hotels many times. Little Willie and I didn't have to worry about tickets for any game. They always had passes for us. On the other hand, when they came to our shows I would always let them in.

Another pastime I mentioned was going to the movies. Every neighborhood had its own movie theater. We had three: (1) the Davison, which showed all cowboy and westerns; (2) the Park, which was also located on Davison near Joseph Campau and Davison Elementary School; and (3) the Lasky Theatre, which was located on Joseph Campau, just South of Davison. The Park and The Lasky showed a variety of movies. Those two were my choice theatres in our neighborhood. Each Friday a new movie would begin running. We usually would go see a movie on that night. We would have our movie-going buddies and we would be with them on the night we would go to see a movie. I had a classmate who lived around the corner from us. She was a young lady who was enormously charming, her name was Vera Highshaw. Vera was very lovely looking. She had a round face with shiny eyes and long black silky beautiful hair which hung down below her shoulders. To make a long story short, she was lovely from head to toe. Vera and I would walk to school together. After I began to work steady, we could not walk from school together because I had to leave school and get to my job. However, we would see each other around the neighborhood. We would talk and play together. Then we started going to the movies together. We spent a lot of time together. For some reason, her parents wanted us to be together and my parents always seemed happy when they saw us together. When she didn't see me coming to pick her up for the walk to the movies, she would walk to our house to get me, then we would leave together.

I remember on one occasion when I went to the movies one Sunday with three of my schoolmate buddies. We went to see a movie at The Lasky Theatre. The theatre was located in our neighborhood on Joseph Campau, just south of Davison Avenue. It was the best theatre of the three in our neighborhood. One of my buddies was carrying a walking cane. We each paid for our tickets at the ticket window then went inside the theatre. When we got inside, a guard saw one of us had a walking cane. The guard was a big White fellow and weighed every bit of 300 pounds. The guard then walked over to my friend and told him he could not bring the came into the theatre. He told him to take it outside and leave it. My buddy said he wasn't going to leave his cane outside. Then the guard tried to take it from him. The guard told him to give him the cane or leave the theatre. Then we all started to leave. The guard told us all to wait. While we were waiting he

Mertis John

called the police. The police came and took us to the Davison Precinct. I was upset all the way. I knew Daddy wouldn't like it at all knowing I was at the police station. The police at the station asked us all a few questions and we explained what had happened. The police said they understood. They knew the guard at the theatre and they also knew that sometimes he took things too far. Then the policemen said we could go. Just as I turned around to leave, who did I see walking towards me? It was Daddy! How did he know that I was here? He asked the police officers if I had done something wrong. They said no, you can take him home. Then we all walked out. When we got outside I told him why we were there. He said that he understood because someone who was at the theatre and saw it all had already told him about it. That's why he had come so quickly to get me.

Another fun thing that we enjoyed was roller skating. The place to roller skate was the Arcadia Roller Rink. We would meet our friends there and make new friends there too. That was one of Little Willie's favorite places. He told me if he had not been successful as an entertainer, he would have pursued skating as a profession. He was a good skater even then.

In those days there were house parties given all around. We would choose the one we thought we would like to go to, depending on who was giving it. The parties were held in someone's basement. The lights would be either blue, red, or yellow. We would dance over and over to the records that were popular at the time. Now when we stepped out to a real dance, it would mean we were going to really prepare for it. We would get permission from the parents of the young lady who we wished to take out that night. To prepare for it, we would make sure our finest outfit would be ready in time because we wanted to look our best. This was because we were taking our dates to the Graystone Ballroom where we would dance to a live band. Sometimes there was a show in addition to the band. We would go to the Graystone Ballroom only on Monday nights because being Black, we were only allowed to go on that night.

Some of our friends who lived near us were Kenny Burrell, who went on to become one of the world's greatest guitarists and the Four Tops Quartet singing group, who later became one of the world's most famous singing groups. The Four Tops recorded many hit records for the Motown Record Company. The group was comprised of Levi Stubbs, Abdul "Duke" Fakir, Renaldo "Obee" Benson, and the late Lawrence Payton. Levi lived closest to us. We lived on the same street. His family and mine were together much of the time. My sister Mildred and his sister Evelyn were running buddies. Willie, myself, and Levi were together a lot. His family loved to sing just as mine did. I suppose that was a factor in the families being as close as we were. My family and his were called cousins. One thing I remember well is that his mother would defend us as quickly as she would her own children. Mildred was a classmate of Duke Fakar of the

My Life and Experiences in the Entertainment World

Four Tops. Also, Willie and Lawrence Payton were classmates for a while. All of us ran in the same circles during those years.

After I got my first car, Willie and my brother Haywood would sometimes go along with me. I would then pick up Levi. We would go for rides in the car. I would drive up Woodward Avenue. We would all start singing as I drove. We would have so much fun singing together. We would get so involved in blending our voices in song and enjoying it so much that before we realized it, we would be in Pontiac, about twenty or so miles north of Detroit. We were enjoying every minute. Between songs Willie would do something funny or tell some funny joke that made us laugh. That all met with Levi's approval too.

Now Willie always demanded attention and he was never still for long. Sometimes he would do things that would be acceptable, and sometimes he would do things that were mischievous. One day in school he decided to hide a girl's glasses who was in his classroom. She must have depended on them very much because the lenses were very strong. After the girl knew they were missing from her desk and she could not find them, she informed the teacher. The teacher in turn, asked all the class to join in looking for them. By this time it was too late for Willie to put them back without being seen. So there was nothing for him to do then but take them home. Looking for the glasses in the room proved to be fruitless. Willie took them home and he began to think. It had been made clear to all of us that we would not be allowed to bring anything home that our parents didn't buy for us. Willie knew he had to invent a story fast. When he walked through the door, he had tears streaming down his cheeks. That's another thing that he could do well…cry when he wasn't really crying. Willie sobbed, "My eyes are giving me trouble. The nurse and the doctor came to school today and they saw my eyes were bothering me so badly that they gave me some glasses to wear."

Daddy knew something was wrong with Willie's story. No one got glasses that quickly, they had to be ordered. Daddy knew that being an honest man, he certainly didn't want us to have anything that was not ours. So Daddy questioned him further but he was not satisfied with the answers he was getting from Willie. Willie had the glasses on all the while and they were giving him a headache because they were prescription very strong lenses. However, he still did not reveal the truth. He had everyone's attention and we felt sorry for him, which he liked.

Later, the principal came by the house. He explained that the glasses were missing and wanted to know if Willie knew where they might be. About that time, Willie walked in wearing the glasses and saw the principal. Willie had been caught but he was glad to give up his headache. We all expected a big whipping to follow, but instead he was punished. Daddy was a strict disciplinarian but the type of discipline he chose this time surprised us all. This time Daddy put him in a burlap sack and hung him so that he was dangling above the floor. He told him he had to stay there until he said that he was sorry for what he had done. Willie was very stubborn and he was no different at this instance. He didn't cry as you may expect, nor did he complain. Instead he sang and prayed. He asked God to bless his mother and father, then continued singing gospel songs. After two hours, Mother Dear called Daddy and asked him to let Willie down. Then Daddy relented and let him down.

There were other instances that led to more visits from school personnel which brought on other punishments to Willie. When they would visit, they were quick to point out how gifted he was, how amazed they were at his intelligence, and how he would focus so much attention on himself. Daddy didn't carry out the punishment he had imposed on Willie completely because many of our arguments were settled by singing. Many times we were told to come together and sing away our madness. We couldn't just go through the motions, we had to do it correctly.

At one time, Mildred and Willie were selling newspapers together. The papers were not selling fast enough for Willie, so he came up with an ingenious idea. He told her he knew how to sell all of these papers fast. "What we're doing now is too slow," he said. "Let's leave a paper at every door then come back later to collect the money. They won't say no when they see the paper." Mildred agreed. Just as Willie had said, when they went back to collect for the papers, everyone paid but they said they hadn't asked for them. "You wouldn't mistreat a kid would you?" asked Willie. We all had a big laugh after that.

Another thing Willie would do was to play blind. He would do this to ride the bus free. This happened several times. He would tell Mildred, "When the bus is almost here, I want you to take my hand and lead me onto the bus and then to a seat." Mildred would put him on the bus, then Willie would ask the driver how much the fare would be. The driver would reply, "The fare for you is free, you're blind." Then Mildred would usher him to a seat. When they would reach their stop and get off the bus, Willie would shout to the driver, "I fooled you. You see, I'm not blind." Then a big laugh would follow.

There was one of our boy friends whom we grew up with that was really blind. His name was Billy Lewis. He played the piano and sang. We would go to his house and sing with him at times. He wanted to be another Ray Charles. Knowing Billy didn't have to pay for riding the bus, that's how Willie came up with the idea to play blind and get the same treatment. Billy's blindness didn't prevent him from living a full and happy life. He cooked and he knew where everything was located in his house. He would dial anyone he cared to talk with and he had several girlfriends he would speak with over the phone almost every day. He could count money as fast as we could. He also showed us how he read Braille. One of the things he enjoyed cooking was chili. He boasted about how well he could make it. My family learned a great deal about blind people from him. He always enjoyed being with us, and we enjoyed being with him.

My Life and Experiences in the Entertainment World

We will never forget the time when some of the family went for an outing at Palmer Park. You can ride bicycles, swim, go on the nature trail, and play baseball, golf, or tennis there. Many picnics and outdoor barbecues are held there too. Also, you could rent a horse and buggy and enjoy a ride around the golf course. Levi Stubbs of the Four Tops was with us that day, as he was on many occasions. The group of us decided to take a buggy ride. Willie wanted to be in control, so we let him. You were not supposed to leave the park, nor even leave the course that had been laid out for the ride. That day Willie, just as he did so many times, wanted to have a little added fun. So as he was driving the buggy, he led the horse out onto Woodward Avenue which is one of our most busiest avenues. He just said, "Hold on. We're going for a good ride." Then he began to make the horse run, which he was not supposed to do. People in cars in the street were blowing their horns and going around the buggy, looking in amazement at what they were seeing. Willie had his fun for the day so he led the horse back onto the trail and to where the ride had started. Willie had run the horse until he was tired and panting. The man in charge of the ponies questioned why the horse was so tired, but everybody got out of the buggy quickly and moved away.

Willie loved several things. If he had any hobbies, they would be in sports. He loved golfing. He also loved roller skating. He loved showing people how good he was at whatever he would do. Bowling was another pastime of his. He loved to try things that were unfamiliar to him, so that he could learn something new. He became good at almost anything he would try. He had tremendous instincts. His instrument was the trumpet. However, he could try any instrument and make sense of it.

Back when Willie was winning amateur contests, Levi Stubbs was also on the stage several times and won first or second prize. They were in competition with each other, but they both enjoyed it. The family was sometimes unaware that he was in the contest until he had won. He and Levi would go to the Paradise Theatre together to be contestants on the same show. They didn't care which of them would win, just as long as one of them won. We all were very close friends.

Chapter Five

Mable Taught Me to Dance
By this time, Mable was attending Pershing High School. In another year I would also be a student at the same high school. Raymond and Toronto were growing up fast and following in the older children's footsteps. Raymond showed us that he also had a love for singing and we could see some talent there. Toronto also loves music and he's learning dance steps fast.

It is understood that all of us love music, singing, and performing. But there are other things that each of us learned. Mable was always good at standing before crowds of people talking and you could see that she liked doing so. She liked getting the attention of an audience while she spoke.

I must give Mable credit for two special things she did for me. When I wanted to dance but couldn't because I hadn't learned, Mable said, "I'm going to teach you to dance tonight." The record "After Hours" was playing. She told me to come on, then she told me how to hold her, and I did. After that, she taught me the dance steps. In a short while, she had me dancing. I'll never forget that night.

Another thing I'll always be grateful to her for is teaching me to type. Mable had typing classes in school. I did not, but I wanted to learn, so Mable told me she would teach me. She would show me each lesson she had learned in class, then show me how to do it. She taught the keyboard to me and how to space and line up, etc. She also taught me all the punctuations. I have never had any typing lessons, except those she gave me at home. From her teaching, I learned to type professional letters and draw up contracts. I typed all of my college papers, and I have also typed the book and manuscripts that have been written by me. I would say that she

My Life and Experiences in the Entertainment World

did a commendable job. It has made lots of things fall into place for me as a result of her teachings.

I was shy until I got older. As a matter of fact, I didn't begin to feel comfortable speaking publicly until I was in college. I didn't feel that I had anything of interest to say publicly until then, but I did enjoy having parts to say in plays. I loved putting my feelings into written words. I had a flair for expressing myself in either songs or poetry. In addition to that, I also loved writing short stories. You could say that writing is one of my greatest loves.

I have always loved horses. I would like to own about four riding horses so that I would have them to enjoy with my family. I am also a lover of sports, I always have been. One other thing that I have desired to do is to work in movies. However, I have never had the opportunity to do so.

Although Haywood never pursued anything other than music, he did enjoy playing baseball. While he was serving in the military, he played in the United States Army Band in Germany. He also did some of the band's arranging. The instruments he played were the tenor and alto saxophones and the clarinet.

Mildred's love was in beauty. After graduating from high school, she enrolled in a beauty school, the Fleming School of Cosmetology, and became a beautician. After working the prescribed period of time in a licensed shop, Mildred opened and operated her own beauty shop on West Warren Avenue for twenty-five years. Mildred also has a love for high fashion clothes and has a wardrobe to satisfy her taste. I have always loved to see her dress. She was a very high class dresser. In keeping with the family's tradition of playing an instrument, she played the piano. Mildred also had a desire to care for the sick. After high school, she studied nursing at Shaw College.

Ernest received good grades in school. Although he did not take to singing as the other members of the family did, he did play the clarinet while in school. After graduating from Northwestern High School, he no longer played. He is the only sibling in the family who didn't sing. Ernest's interest was sports. Baseball was his favorite, he played the game every chance he got. It was said he loved to play baseball more than he loved to eat.

Of the three sisters in the family, Delores is the youngest. Delores liked to sing and early on she did have some aspirations to have a career as a singer. She sang at a few clubs around the city and at various affairs in the area, but she didn't continue to pursue a career.

Raymond is the fifth son in the family. He loved music, singing, and sports just as the rest of us do. Later in life he enjoyed his three children; two sons and one daughter.

Toronto is the sixth boy and the ninth child of Mertis and Lillie John Sr. He had a special gift of dancing and enjoyed any chance he got to do so. Later he started playing drums. He also enjoyed going out with his older brothers and sisters. Sometimes when he would ask to go with me when I was attempting to go somewhere private, he would sneak in the car

Mertis John

before me. He would then hide in the back on the floor and I didn't know he was in the car until I had driven some distance away or reached my destination. It would only make me laugh when I would discover what he had done.

Toronto graduated from Northwestern High School. Going back to the time when he was five and six years old, he would accompany Willie while he was on stage and at his television appearances around the city, across the river and border between the United States and Canada, and in Windsor, Canada. Some of the television shows that he danced on were "The Ed Mackenzie Show," "Robin Seymour," and "The Chuck Davie's Show" which were seen from Canada on Channel 9. When Toronto became eligible for the military draft, he was inducted and he served in the U.S. Army. When he returned home, he continued his education and he enrolled in college.

Chapter Six

I continued to work at the wash rack, or car wash if you please, until I was eighteen years old and in my senior year at Pershing High School.

My father had been working at the Dodge Main Plan on Jos. Campau for many years at that time. In the summers when I was much younger I would sometimes ride the streetcar with him to the job. He would get off at the plant, and I would continue on to the end of the line, turn around, and go back home. He had told me many times that when I became old enough, he was going to bring me to the plant to work with him. I had told him time and time again, that I would never do that type of work. But still, he insisted that I go to the plant with him to work, knowing all the time that I was already working and that I didn't want to do the type of work that he did.

It was the month of June and school vacation had started. Daddy came into my room and said, "I'm taking you to the plant today to be hired for work." I reminded him that I already had a job and that I didn't want to go and work at an auto plant. This was on Monday. He repeated this same scenario for the next four days. But on Friday of that week, he told me that he had already promised his boss that I wanted employment there and that I would be reporting on that week. They were looking for me to come today. I didn't want to be employed there, but my father wanted me to be employed where he was employed. His reasons were never explained to me. He had already asked them if I could come to work there and they told him, "Yes, just bring him in and we'll hire him." So with that, reluctantly, I gave my consent. But only so that he could keep his word with them.

Mertis John

So he took me to the plant and we headed straight to the employment line. The line, I remember, was very long. I stepped behind the last person in the line, willing to wait my turn. Then Daddy said, "Come on, follow me." The line extended from inside of the employment office to the outside onto the sidewalk at the street. Daddy took me past everyone right on up to the counter. He spoke to one of the men behind the counter and he handed him a piece of paper. The man then gave him an application form and told him to give it to me and have me fill it out and bring it back to him. Daddy handed the application to me. I filled it out and took it to the man at the counter. He read the answers that I had supplied.

"That's good," said the man. He asked me to have a seat and soon sent someone to direct me to the Medical Department. I gave the nurse the paper which had an okay for me to have my physical. I had the physical and the doctor gave me another piece of paper to take back to the man in the Employment Office indicating I had passed.

I went back to the Employment Office and showed the man that I had passed my physical. Then he asked me if I had brought my birth certificate. I told him no. He said, "Go home and get it and bring it back to me." I went home, got the birth certificate, and took it to him to see. He said, "That's fine." His next question was, "When do you want to start work?"

I was totally surprised. I didn't know what to say. I asked, "When do I have to start?"

He said, "When you want to."

"Can I just start Monday?" I asked.

He said, "Sure. I'll give you this card. Bring it in Monday when you come to work. Come in a little early and go to window number twenty, give the man this card and he will give you your badge." Just like that, I had a job in an automobile factory in one day without asking. I had a job in a place where I had never planned to work. It was all because Daddy wanted me to work there. He never told me why.

On Monday, I went in early to pick up my badge. I had been assigned to work the third shift. I would start at 11:00 P.M. and work to 7:00 A.M. That too, was arranged by my father. He was considering the fact that I was still a student in my senior year in high school. He had asked them to schedule my work hours so that I could continue working there when I returned to school in the Fall.

When I arrived for my first work day in the plant, someone was waiting to take me to my department. I would be working in Department 101 and my badge number was 141, the same department my father worked in. He worked the second shift from 3:00 P.M. to 11:00 P.M. I saw him when I was being taken to the office to meet my foreman and to get my first job assignment that night. He met me at the office. Surprisingly, many of the men already knew who I was when I walked into the department. I was later taken to my job by the man who would be my foreman. That department was very large. I was told more than 1,500 people worked in that

My Life and Experiences in the Entertainment World

department alone, over the span of three shifts. We worked on some of the main engine parts, including the motor block, the motor cylinder head, and the fly wheel. Our jobs were to mill, grind, ream, and prepare the block to take on the other internal parts that make up an automobile engine.

My first job was to catch the block, take it off a conveyor after it had gone through an oil process, then stack them on a flat skid where they would be taken to engine department, number 105, located next to ours. After a few days of doing that job, I was then moved to a machine which I learned to operate in short order. It was a machine which drilled several holes into the block simultaneously. I enjoyed operating that machine. I got to know it, and the machine began to know that it was I who was running it. On the move to the machine, I received a five-cent raise. Each time you were moved up to anything more difficult or if it was deemed more important, you would be compensated by receiving a raise of five cents per hour. My starting salary had been $1.79 per hour. There was also a shift premium of five cents per shift on the second and third shifts. That means the job that I was doing paid me ten cents more than the man doing the same job on the day shift. I was elevated up to jobs quite rapidly. Of course, there was a raise with each one. I really didn't want to move from the first machine. I had come to love it. But this was happening I believe, because of my father's being there and because of his good work record. He told me to accept each move, and I did. Subsequently, I learned to run every job in that department.

I continued to work at the automobile factory after I returned to school in September and completed my high school education. I would work from 11:00 P.M. to 7:00 A.M. I had a first-hour class. That meant after I left the job, I had one hour to get to school and into my classroom. My schedule was very tight, but I made it every day on time. Sometimes I had to fight off sleepiness, but I remained alert. I was determined to accomplish my goal.

After I had held this job for six months, I purchased my first new car. I'll never forget the day I drove my first brand new car home! It was November 27. I had ordered the car earlier and it had been delivered to the dealer for me to come in and pick it up. That first car was a Mercury. I didn't know which car I should buy at first. After thinking it over and going over the various new cars, I decided I should buy a Mercury. Being a minor and not of age at the time, I had to have my father co-sign for the car. I also had to have him co-sign for the car insurance. He did both, and he was proud to do so. Having this car made me more popular in my neighborhood as well as around the school. After I purchased this first new car, I had trouble with the police seemingly at every turn. At that time, the police in Detroit was ninety-five percent White. It became a regular occurrence for the police to stop me for no reason, except that I was Black and driving a new car. When they would see me, a Black boy driving a new car, they would pull me over. Then they would proceed to throw out everything in the glove compartment and pull out all of the seats. Then they would ask, "Whose car is this?" I would tell them that it was mine. Then they would ask, "How did you get it?"

I would answer, "I bought it."

Then they would ask, "Where do you work?" and I would tell them.

All that was done only to harass me because I'm Black. They never found anything out of order because there was nothing that I was doing wrong. I was never given an apology for tearing out my car, nor did they ever put anything back in place. They would go back to their car laughing.

In June of the next year, I graduated from Pershing High School as a member of the National Honor Society, and with honors in Music. In September of that year, I enrolled at Wayne University to continue my education. It didn't require my leaving home. The school is located in the central part of the city which made it easy in terms of having to work and attend school at the same time. Not having to be away from home was great. The only way that I could attend school was to work as well. After I went to work at the wash rack when I was twelve, I began to take care of myself. There was no way that I could continue school unless I supported it with the funds that I earned. After I had worked at the car wash for a period of four months, I became independent enough to take care of myself. Daddy no longer took care of me. I took that responsibility myself. I paid rent, bought my clothes, and put myself through school.

At the same time, the family was continuing to do our music thing. We were singing and Willie was still doing his solo thing as often as he could. Haywood and I were still playing our horns. We would play in our church and wherever else we could.

Soon after, a minister named Reverend Folmer who heard me play in church, asked if I could accompany him as he traveled to different places holding revivals. I asked my parents if I could go and play for him and they gave their permission. In the meantime, he also got permission from my mother. We traveled in his car to places like Mount Clemens, Pontiac, Flint, Saginaw, Muskegon, and Toledo, Ohio. I wasn't paid much, but I was young and I was able to play my horn, so I was happy.

He drove a Ford. I can remember hearing him say that the car swayed at times when the wind was high. However, he would go on to say, "I know how to keep it on the road."

During those years, Detroit and Windsor (the city just across the river from Detroit in Canada) would celebrate what was known as "The Emancipation Freedom Festival." During the course of the celebration, many entertainers from this area, Canada, and the United States would perform at the festival. It was a very colorful event. In addition to entertainment on stage, there were parades with cars and horses. There was dancing and the Canadian bagpipers were always very colorful. It would always conclude at Jackson Park in Windsor. That's where the stage shows

My Life and Experiences in the Entertainment World

would be held. There were a variety of foods on hand which were sold. It was always a happy, fun-filled time.

On this year, the show's promoter, Mr. Washington, asked my parents if Willie could be in the show. They consented. Other artists performing were: Jackie Wilson, Hank Ballard, and the Midnighters. Joseph Hunter played the piano and other keyboards for the Midnighters. He later became the Artist and Repertoire director of my company, Meda Records, years later. Also performing in the show were: The Royal Jokers, Billy Lewis, The Four Tops, and the list went on.

While on the subject of Canada, I would like to say just a little more about it since it's located so close to my home. There was a time when I crossed the river into Windsor, Ontario, to shop for food each week. While we have territories which we call states, in Canada the same type areas are known as provinces. Toronto, the largest and most popular city in the southern part of Canada, is located about 175 miles north of Windsor, Ontario. I took my son Darryl there for the first time when he was eight or nine years old for a vacation which he enjoyed. We also traveled in the country of Canada doing shows. In my opinion, the most beautiful cities in Canada are Vancouver, British Columbia, on the west coast and Toronto on the east coast.

As we continued to grow up, we were going to school, singing, and having the kind of fun that the other children in our neighborhood were having. But now we were meeting lots of people whom we had not known in the entertainment circle. More people were paying attention to Willie's singing and asking my parents to allow him to appear on their shows. One popular promoter of shows in the area then was Homer Jones. He would have Willie on every show he promoted in the area. Shows were held at the Rogers Theatre on West Warren Avenue, the Warfield Theatre on Hastings Street, the Gold Coast Theatre on Grand River Avenue, the Broadway Capitol Theatre on Broadway (downtown), the Park Theatre on East Davison Avenue, the United Artist Theatre (downtown), the Graystone Ballroom, the Veterans Memorial Auditorium on West Jefferson Avenue, and other show places not mentioned here. But I can't leave the one and only Paradise Theatre on Woodward Avenue out.

Chapter Seven

The Family Sees a Transition

Things changed for the family. Willie performed more and more as a single act. We very rarely sang as the group that always performed together in the past years. When celebrities would come to town, many would seek out Willie to join them and their band on the road. Some of the bands who had an interest in him were Lionel Hampton, Dizzy Gillespie, and others.

Willie could easily have chosen other professions if he had desired. But entertaining was his God-given talent. He showed class and professionalism at an early age. He was really a creative genius, a man ahead of his time. I truly regret that he did not live out his full potential. He was a very talented and astute person. Early on, when the band leaders would come to our home to ask my parent's permission to let Willie go on the road as the band singer, the answer was always "no." My parents insisted he was too young, and they wanted him to remain in school. Our parents were not impressed with the possibility that Willie could go out on the road with big name bands at that time. That would come later.

Later that year, Mother Dear went to visit our relatives in New Orleans, just as she would do from time to time. It was the month of August. While she was away, I really got the surprise of my life. I received a letter from the President of the United States. It was a letter informing me that I was to be inducted into the Armed Forces and that I was to go to the Induction Center on a certain day. Here I was, out of high school by about a year and a half, going to college and minding my own business. Now the government was calling me. I showed the letter to my dad. He

My Life and Experiences in the Entertainment World

asked me if I wanted to go. I told him no. He told me that he didn't want me to go either. He didn't have to serve in military service.

I could hardly wait for Mother Dear to return from New Orleans. It seemed that she was taking forever to return. When she finally did, I was really glad to see her. I told her about the letter, and we discussed it. However, she didn't show any emotions while we talked, nor did she afterwards. I began to prepare for what was to be my destiny with the Armed Forces.

I didn't know whether to sell my car or to leave it with my father. I finally decided to leave it at home with my father. I left my baseballs, bats, and gloves with my brother Haywood and my bicycle with my brother Willie. Days finally passed and it was time for me to leave home for the military service. The first step was to go to the Induction Center to be examined for the military service. If I should pass, I would be inducted on this very day. I went to bed the night before leaving, but I didn't really have a good night's sleep. I was restless, wondering just what would transpire on the following day. I awakened early the next morning not knowing fully, what to expect. No one was up or even got up before I left that morning. Although I'm sure Mother and Daddy were awake all along, but didn't want me to know. They knew I was sad and didn't want to leave my family or my home and go to some faraway place to live the life of a soldier.

When I prepared to leave, I went to my mother and father's room. The door was closed but they both said at the same time, "Come in." I told them that I was ready to leave. We said our goodbyes. Then they said, "You'd better go now so that you won't be late." I prayed to God that he would send me back home. I went out the door, gave my car a long look, then walked on to the bus stop and waited for the bus to come. I was to get the bus, ride downtown, and then take a second bus that would take me to Fort Wayne where I would have my examination and possible induction.

I finally arrived at Fort Wayne. I was directed by soldiers in the camp as to where I was to go. When I got inside, I saw fellows that I knew. One in particular was Doyle Myrick. We had lived near each other and we had been classmates, too. He wasn't taking it as hard as I. We decided to stay together as long as we could. Many doctors examined us that day. In the end, both of us passed. Doyle's older brother, Wilbert, whom I also knew, was already in service and had told Doyle a lot about being a soldier. Doyle said he would also teach me. That made me feel somewhat better.

At that point, I could see that I would not be returning home that day or anytime soon. Late that afternoon, they loaded us onto buses and took us up to Fort Custer near Battle Creek, Michigan. When we arrived, it was later in the evening between 7:00 P.M. and 8:00 P.M. The mess hall was closed so what they gave us to eat was next to nothing. They apologized but that was no relief for our hungry stomachs. They then told us to fall out and then they marched us to the quarter master where they threw our duffel bags and uniforms to us, which in a number of cases did not fit. We were also given bedding at the same time. Then we marched back to a barracks

Mertis John

where we made up our bunks and bedded down for our first night in the service of our country. Doyle and I bedded downside by side and we continued to do so until we were shipped out to our training bases a week later. During that period of time, Doyle, just as he had promised, taught me things that he had learned from his brother, Wilbert. I wish we could have been together throughout our tenure in the service. I remember there was one thing that I refused to do during my initial days in the service, salute an officer. I just couldn't bring myself to do it. I felt that no person was higher or more important than another, I still feel the same. I avoided saluting by going in the opposite direction and not getting face-to-face with officers. I was successful at it during the time I spent at Fort Custer, but that was only a week or so. At the time I didn't realize you salute the person's position, not the individual. It's a part of the military's training and disciplining military personnel.

I had left home seven days before now, but on the seventh day which was the first Sunday that I had been away, I had visitors. My sister Mildred, my brother Willie, and my girlfriend had traveled with my cousin Josh to see me. I was very pleased to see them all. I just wished that their stay could have been longer, or better still, that I could have gone back home with them, but that didn't happen. Two or three days after they had visited me, we received our orders to report to our assigned training camps. My friend Doyle and I were about to be separated. I was sent to Camp Pickett in Virginia to take infantry and medical training. Doyle was sent to Fort McClellan in Alabama to take infantry and chemical training. We were put on a train that had sections assigned to the military personnel. Fortunately, the train would travel to Detroit and make a layover stop. I called home to let my family know that I would be making the stop. When we arrived in Detroit, some of my family was there to meet me at the station. I don't recall who all, but I do know that I was very happy to be home, even for that very short time.

After what seemed to be a very, very short time at the station, it was time for us to board our trains to our training camps. Doyle traveled to Alabama and we didn't see each other again until we were out of the service. However, we did write each other. I went on to Virginia to receive my basic training. After I arrived at Camp Pickett, I saw that it was impossible for me to avoid saluting officers. The inevitable had caught up with me at last. It was part of our training.

I began my training and finally got through it as all soldiers had done before me. By the time I was finished, I was a prepared soldier and I felt that I was ready for combat. I had been drafted because of the Korean War, at the time it was the height of the war. Now it was told to us that many fierce battles were being fought and many casualties were being inflicted on both sides.

I finished my training in the month of March. I was happy to get it all behind me. Soldiers were needed to go to Korea as fast as possible to

My Life and Experiences in the Entertainment World

replace those who had suffered casualties. After training we were told we were needed in Korea and that was where we were going. About 80 percent of all the soldiers drafted during that period saw action in the Korean War. I was one of them.

Since we were so desperately needed, we were permitted only fourteen days to come home and be with our families before we would have to continue on to the designated facility where we would be shipped out by boat to the war zone, Korea.

At this time, we turned the things we were to leave behind in to the quarter master. Then we packed our duffel bags with our uniforms and personal items that we would be keeping. We loaded onto a post bus that would take us to the train station in the little, southern, country town of Blackstone, Virginia. At the train station, I happily jumped off the bus and checked in for the train that would take me home. The train ride took a few hours. I don't remember the exact time. However, I do remember arriving at Michigan Central Station in the late evening. I was extremely happy to be back home for the next fourteen days.

Everyone was glad to see me and I was certainly happy to see each one of them. They were asking how long I would be home and where I would be going next. I knew that I would subsequently go on to Korea after leaving California, but I just told them that I would be going to California next. Daddy wanted to know if I had started smoking yet. We had made a bet before leaving home that I would start smoking while I was in service. "No," I told him I still was not smoking and I was sure I would not start to smoke. He told me that all soldiers smoked and that I would be smoking the next time that he saw me. I told him he was wrong, I would not. So the bet continued.

The twelve or fourteen days that I spent at home passed very fast. Now this was my last day before I would be leaving for Camp Stoneman in California. I got the car, then drove to my girlfriend's house. I picked her up and we proceeded to Belle Isle. We got something to eat and gazed at each other and at the stars for hours. I didn't want the evening to end because I knew this was my last night at home for a long time. Tomorrow I would be going far, far away. The night did come to an end. The morning came. I had to take the car back to my parent's house, leave it, get my bags, then go to the train station. We said our goodbyes, then I boarded the train.

Chapter Eight

After I had boarded the train the pullman came and directed me to my compartment. Everything was paid by the government. The trip had been pre-scheduled. I had been given the travel voucher and meal tickets. I had the best of everything all the way to California. All I had to do was sign my name. My compartment was private. I watched the lovely scenery by day and my bed was made for me at night. I ate the best meals available in the club car. It was like not being in the military service at all, and for awhile I forgot that I was. The trip took three days.

When we arrived in California, the other soldiers and I were taken by bus to Camp Stoneman in Richmond (not far from San Francisco). While there, we were given a little advanced training. But mostly, we only heard lectures about what to expect in combat and how best to survive. We were told to fall out for every formation to see if we were on orders to ship out. The formations were usually called twice daily, morning and in the evening. As ordered, I would fall out for every formation. After almost a week of falling out two or three times a day, my name never came up on the roster to ship out. After this formation, I went to the sergeant to see if there had been a mistake or if I had been forgotten. He said no, there was no mistake and that I was not forgotten.

There was a very nice restaurant on the post that served a civilian menu. I went there that evening for my supper. After I had finished eating and was about to leave, a man told me that he needed help there and asked if I could come to work. He told me what he needed and I told him I would come in the next day. The next day I fell out for the morning formation. Again, my name was not on the list to ship out. I walked to the restaurant

My Life and Experiences in the Entertainment World

and told the man I was ready to start work. I worked that day and every day after until my name came up on the list to ship out. It took at least two weeks for them to cut ship out orders for me. I began to feel that they were going to let me remain there in California. I was wishing they would. However, it all came to an end. I received orders to fall out and prepare to be transported to the San Francisco Harbor, which isn't far from the camp. At San Francisco, we would embark on our ship which was the USS Meigs and start our long voyage across the largest of the oceans, the Pacific Ocean.

I was taken to the area where we were checked and tagged, then we were told to walk up the gangplank onto the ship. It was a troop ship and it was carrying 5,000 U.S. Troops. It was a little past noon when I boarded the ship, but we didn't pull away until almost dark. The voyage took fourteen days to complete before we landed in Japan. For the two weeks we were at sea, I was assigned to the laundry. I had no experience at it, but they had me running a pressing machine. I had to press the uniforms of all the Navy personnel on board the ship. The uniforms would first go through the machine cleaning process and then I would press them to a first class look. We were under Naval orders until we landed in Japan. As we prepared to dock, our orders again came from Army personnel. We docked and were told to prepare to debark. After we left the ship, we were assembled in groups. The roll was called then we were driven to a camp not far from Tokyo. I was there for one week. While there, we were given a little advanced training. It was certain then that I was on my way to Korea where a hot war was raging. On the following Saturday, I received my orders to go to my assigned outfit in Korea. We were again loaded onto trucks and taken to the harbor where we boarded a ship in Yokohama and sailed on to Korea. Sometime the next day, which was Sunday, we landed at Pusan. After we landed and debarked, we were assembled and accounted for. After that we were loaded onto a train and taken up north so that we could join our assigned outfits. I was assigned to be part of the 52nd Medical Battalion.

Korea was known as the land of the frozen chosen. At the time I was there, there was no sign of it ever having any significant amount of industrial development. It is a land of mountainous terrain. It is mostly a farming country where primitive methods are employed to grow rice, their chief product. The farmers were mostly peasants. The country has an awful smell which takes no time at all to discover. The reason for this is because in growing their crops, human manure is used for fertilizing. They use wagons drawn by oxen to collect the manure, the same oxen they use to plow the land. Also, chopping and weeding their crops is done the primitive way, by hand, using hand hoes. The manure was collected twice daily, early in the mornings and again in the evenings. Anytime they were making their collections, the smell would get stronger. There are rice fields everywhere you see a farm, and they are numerous all over the country.

Mertis John

The nation of Korea itself is a country in East Asia which has been divided since 1948 into two states. The People's Democratic Republic of Korea is in the north. Its population is approximately 10,930,000, and its capital is Pyongyang. The Republic of Korea is in the south. Its population is approximately 28,155,000, and the capital is Seoul. The territory is just south of Russia, and it borders the country of China. The Korean War lasted three years, from 1950 to 1953.

After I settled in with my new company, I wrote home to let everyone know where I was and that I was fine. I was hoping that I would hear from home real soon. As a medic, I was one of those who attended the sick and wounded. I fell into my routine gradually. My mail finally caught up with me and I was kept abreast of what was happening back home. After I had been in Korea six or eight months, I was allowed to go on R& R. I went to Tokyo for a week.

I had heard many times that the Korean War referred to as a conflict. It is the war which followed less than five years after the World War II ended. How dare anyone refer to the Korean War as a conflict! From the White House to the Pentagon, to the man on the street, from 1950–1953 there was a war in Korea, the Korean War! The United States was involved in a dominant way.

The war was brought on by North Korea's invasion of South Korea. It raged for three years as the United States' troops and forces, along with troops from 15 other nations, responded to a request for help by the United Nations and tried to repel the invaders from the north. The war broadened in 1951 with the entry of Communist China taking sides with North Korea. The war ended with a cease-fire agreement.

It is said the war caused more than 800,000 casualties and approximately $3 billion worth of property damage. For a decade thereafter, a huge United States aid effort, together with international assistance, was directed towards providing food and shelter, repairing war damage, and laying the groundwork for an eventual economic development of South Korea.

Not too long following my assignment to Korea, as the months passed, an entrepreneur by the name of Harry Balk, who owned theaters in Detroit, saw Willie perform. From that moment on he began to pursue Willie, to record and sign him to a performing contract. He said then, "I want him."

But he was warned, "Don't claim him just yet. You'll have to get past his father first and that may not be so easy."

"But I've got to sign him. He's the only real true entertainer that I have seen for a long time," he said. Willie had not yet reached his fifteenth birthday and would not until November 15th of that year. "He's got what it takes to be a star," Harry went on. After Willie's performance, Harry introduced himself to Willie and told him he would like to manage his career. So Willie took Harry home with him to meet our parents and to discuss management with them.

My Life and Experiences in the Entertainment World

At that first meeting, Harry was not given permission to takeover management of Willie. However, Harry persisted. He made several trips to the John home. Finally, Daddy was ready to let Willie further his gift of singing and performing and an agreement was struck. My parents signed the agreement after it was drawn up and after Daddy's lawyer had read and approved it. At that, Harry Balk was Willie's manager and in control of his career.

Harry wanted a record out on Willie as soon as possible. The Christmas season was approaching. Harry began to think about a Christmas release. He came across a Christmas song with the story line of a child asking his mom a question, "Mommy What Happened to Our Christmas Tree?" A song with a story that would fit his young, new-found star perfectly since Willie was just a teenager. Harry gave Willie the song which was to be his first commercial record release. Harry's initial investment on Willie paid for the production of this release. The record was released on the independent label, Prize Records. That initial release was a good starter. It sold about 200,000 copies. For the first time, Willie had a chance to leave home and go on the road and sing for new audiences and see how they responded to him. Also, to meet new people. This swing took him to New York, Baltimore, Washington, and other cities in that vicinity. Willie was accompanied on this tour by his manager, Harry Balk.

After this tour ended, Harry and Willie returned home. He didn't have another tour for a while. However, he did various shows around home. He was also doing guest appearances on many other shows when they came into town.

Before the next Christmas I would be home. Well, that news finally came when it was time for me to return to the United States and eventually make my way back home. When the time arrived, I went to Pusan by truck, then I boarded a ship, the *USS Collins*, for the voyage back home. The *USS Collins* was a much better looking vessel than the *USS Meigs* which had brought me over. After we left Korea, we had to go to Tokyo to pick up some other military personnel who were also returning to the United States.

The ship was finally loaded and we were pulled away from the dock by a tug. We were happily on our way home. From the time we left Japan until we landed in Seattle, Washington, we counted twelve days. After we landed at the Port of Seattle and walked off the ship onto United States soil, I felt as if I was walking on air. The feeling of being back in your own country after going through the ordeal of that recent past is indescribable. To say that I was happy to be back on homeland would be an understatement.

We were assembled in groups and were called out by name and directed to board trucks to be taken to our processing station, Fort Lawton, near Seattle. There we began the process of being discharged from service. We were taken through five days of processing at Fort Lawton. At its completion, we were flown by military aircraft to our army areas for separation, which for me was Fort Sheridan, outside Chicago. On our flight to Fort

Mertis John

Sheridan, each of us was given an opportunity to sit at the controls with the captain and fly the plane. We were on our way home and as an added pleasure, we were allowed to get the feel of flying the plane. That was a real thrill for me because I had always loved airplanes and had dreamt of learning to fly. So this added to the excitement of returning home.

We finally arrived at the airport outside Chicago. We were then taken to Fort Sheridan where I was to be separated from the military service. After arriving there, we began to go through the usual procedures for being discharged. Going to the doctors, listening to lectures by officers and others asking us to remain in service, offering promotions if we did, getting our service records in order, and finally our meeting with the chaplain. For me, it was all routine. I knew what I was going to do, go back home and get back into music again. My brother Willie and I had already been discussing the possibility of my writing songs for him when I returned home. That is one of the things I did when I got back home.

My stay at Fort Sheridan, if my memory is correct, lasted five days and I was then given my discharge from military service. I don't remember at this point, how I got to downtown Chicago. However, I do remember that I went to the train station and boarded the train which would take me home. I arrived at the Michigan Central Station in Detroit that evening. I had told my family that I would be coming home that day, but I didn't give any time. I didn't really know the time that I would be leaving Chicago's station, nor the time of my arrival in Detroit. So no one meet me at the station, which was fine. I wanted to surprise everyone. I got a cab home.

I remember everyone was surprised when they saw me. Also, I remember Willie was not home when I arrived. I kept looking and waiting for him to come in. After a while, he finally did come in. Just like him, he always had some place to go and someone to see. When he came in and saw me, the first thing he said was, "Hey, man!" in an unfamiliar voice. During the years which I was away in the service, Willie's voice had changed. It was nothing unusual. It was however, something that I had not thought about in relation to Willie. I had to also get used to the street talk that he had taken up while I was away.

We began to talk about different things that had taken place while I was away. He tried to bring me up to date as best he could. Then my sister Mildred asked, "Aren't you going to check your car tonight?" I told her no, I would wait until tomorrow. I had left the car for Daddy to drive and take care of until I returned, so that the family would have transportation. The next morning I went out to drive the car for the first time since returning home. I found that the car had not been taken care of. Consequently, it didn't operate well. A considerable amount of money would have to be spent to get it back in good running condition. In the meantime, I did what I had to do to keep it running. Then I decided it would be in my best interest to buy a new car. I decided I would buy a 98 Oldsmobile. So I visited an Oldsmobile dealer. We discussed a deal and

My Life and Experiences in the Entertainment World

when we came to an agreement, I gave him a down payment. Then I asked him to order the car I wanted from the manufacturer and he did. I kept driving what had been my first new car, which was a Mercury, until the Oldsmobile was built and delivered to the dealer. I had to wait about four or five weeks before the new car was ready and delivered.

In the meantime, Willie wanted me to meet his manager, Harry Balk, who had been acquired while I was away in the service. So Willie had me go meet Harry along with him. Harry told me he had wanted to meet me too because he had heard that I was a songwriter. We talked business for a good while in our first meeting.

MEDA RECORDS **MERTIS JOHN**

Chapter Nine

I received a call from my automobile salesman few days before Christmas telling me that the car I had ordered was in and that I could pick it up the next day. That was good news! I went in and took ownership of the car on December 23.

At this time, the group of my brothers and sisters who had sung together for so long was no longer a group. Haywood was still away in service in Germany, Willie had become a full-fledged single act, Mable was an adult had her own place, so we were going in different directions.

We enjoyed a lovely Christmas together that year, my first Christmas back home. We were all home together except Haywood who was still away in military service. Willie continued his performing in and around Detroit. As big name attractions would come in to play gigs, Willie would be added to many of the shows. This continued for another five or six months. Then Paul Williams came to town to do a show. Willie played on the gig with him. Paul had made a dance record called the "Huckle Buck" famous a few years earlier. There was the song to go along with the dance as well. After this gig was over, Paul Williams wanted Willie to go on the road with him, so Willie asked our parents for permission. That prompted a meeting between Paul and our parents. Mother and Daddy consented to allow Willie to leave home and travel with Paul Williams and his band. They asked Paul to take care of Willie. He promised them that he would, so when Paul left Detroit to continue his tour, Willie was with him as his band vocalist. We all knew that performing would be the only career that Willie would be satisfied doing. We also understood how talented Willie was and that he really enjoyed performing. Also, we wanted him to be successful in his career.

Mertis John

Willie's dream was not just to be another singer. He wanted to be, from deep down inside his soul, what our parents had wanted us to be…the best in whatever we did. Willie wanted to be the best. This is why he could not be content at just singing around home. He knew that he had to travel the world and perform for the people of the world. Moreover, he wanted to be a recording star.

This tour didn't net Willie large sums of money, but it did lay a foundation for what was to come a little later in his career. Not having a track record performing away from home and not having a current record that was being played on the radio attributed to an artist being on the lower pay scale. At that point, Willie was having that experience. But on the other hand, more audiences were seeing him perform and got to see how well he performed, and they didn't forget the next time he came to their towns. Soon he would have a current record that was being played on the radio. That would get them anxious to come see him perform and he would be paid a considerable amount higher than he received the previous time around.

Finally, the tour with Paul Williams ended in New York City. After the last show of this tour ended. Paul was going to see that Willie returned home, but Willie begged him not to send him home. He wanted to remain in New York for a while for he was sure he would be able to sign on with a good record company if he could just get an audition. Also, he had told Mother Dear that he would not return home until he had a recording contract and a new record on the market. Well, this led to calling home. Willie called home to let our parents know the tour had ended in New York, but he wanted to remain there a while to see some people who may be interested in signing him to a recording contract. My parents knew how badly Willie wanted a contract with a good company, so they told Mr. Williams it would be alright to leave Willie in New York. Willie, very determined to be successful in the career he had chosen, said to Mother Dear once more, "I'll be home when I have a record on the market. Don't worry about me, I'll make it. I'm all right."

So Willie was left in New York City, the entertainment capitol of the world. This is where he wanted to be. Here, he would be able to see and meet the people who could help him build his career. Mr. Williams didn't want to leave Willie behind and he was astonished at by our parents giving permission to leave him in New York. However, he did leave him in New York when he left. Willie had the utmost determination to do just as he had said he would do. Shortly after Willie had been left in New York alone, he went to the office of King Record Company. There he met and became acquainted with Mr. Henry Glover who was the A&R Director of the company. Willie asked for an audition that day without being scheduled to audition. It just so happened that Mr. Glover was recording a singer that night who had written a song for himself. The singer was Titus Turner and the song was "All Around the World." The session got underway. However, Titus, for some reason, just couldn't get the song right. But Willie was

My Life and Experiences in the Entertainment World

there watching and listening to everything that was taking place. He suddenly got up and said, this is the way you want to do it. Everyone stopped and listened to Willie do the song from top to bottom, from beginning to end, to everyone's amazement. At that point, Titus said he couldn't sing that song but Willie could. Willie had a very unusual keenness for learning a song fast. That's what he had done in this situation. He had learned the song he had just heard in no time flat. He also knew the style in which he could sing it.

That changed the session around completely. Mr. Glover, at that moment, told Willie he would like for him to record the song. He then cut the song with Willie. He liked what he heard. Those were the days of the 78 RPM records. They had the "A" side of the record. Now he needed to come up with the "B" side. Having had no recording schedule for Willie, Mr. Glover had no idea what he would use for the "B" side. Willie told him not to worry, he had a song that he had written and it could be used for the "B" side. Mr. Glover wanted to hear it. Then Willie sung it for him. It's entitled, "Don't Leave Me Dear." After hearing it, Mr. Glover liked the song and said it would be a good choice for the "B" side. Mr. Glover told the arranger, Mr. Andy Gipson, to work out the charts for the song for the session's musicians to play. Willie ran the song down to Andy so that he could get the correct key and style to arrange the song in. Also, to get the correct moves Willie would be making in order to get a good feel in the chart arrangement.

With that, Willie was almost set with his first major release. Andy finished the arrangements on the songs. Mr. Glover got the musicians together again and Willie was ready to do his thing in the sound booth. Willis Jackson did the fine work on tenor saxophone on one of those recordings. Andy ran it down with the musicians, then Mr. Glover got a balance on the recording boards. Then he was to set to roll for the take. This recording session was finished in short order. The mastering of both sides was done and the recording was completed. The master was then ready to be taken to the record plant to be pressed and then shipped to disc jockeys all over the country for air play and to the distributors all over the country so that the record stores could purchase them to sell in their stores to the record buyers.

Fortunately, King Records owned its record plant and distributors in the various cities. At the record plant in Cincinnati, it was equipped to press 30,000 records per day and ship them. At that time, there were only one or two other record companies who had similar operations. So Willie was very blessed to be with King Records. Oh, was he really! Aside from Willie John, other popular artists who were signed to King Records at that time were Charles Brown, Earl Bostic, James Brown, Bill Doggett, Hank Ballard and The Midnighters, The Five Royals, The Charms, Annie Laurie, and Billy Ward and The Dominos, to name a few.

Charles Brown is known for his recording the Christmas standard, "Merry Christmas Baby," Earl Bostic for many beautiful instrumental

Mertis John

recordings, and The Charms for "Gum Drop," The Five Royals are famous for "This Is Dedicated to the One I Love." Bill Doggett, organist and band leader is famous for "Honky Tonk," "Hold It" and more. He also played on Willie John's "Suffering with the Blues," and "Heart Break (It's Hurting Me)." James Brown is famous for many recordings, "Try Me," "Please, Please, Please," and it goes on and on. Annie Laurie's big one was "It Hurts to Be in Love." Hank Ballard was the person who wrote and recorded the monster hit, "The Twist." Many people believed that Chubby Checker wrote it. No, he only recorded it after Hank got it going. The people at his company thought it would be good to cover it, which they did.

I happened to be in the studio the night that Hank first cut "The Twist." After the session ended, he was elated. His words were, "I know I have a big one here." Hank, you were so right. One of the biggest dance craves of all times was started with that record–your record "The Twist."

Even though the recording was completed and ready for pressing, Willie was still a minor, just sixteen years old. So Mr. Glover and Sid Nathan, the owner of the company, had to wait and see if they really had the star that they envisioned to have in Willie. Willie first had to have the contract approved and signed by our parents. So Willie called home to speak with Mother Dear and give her the news in reference to what had transpired between him and the record company. First Willie talked to Mother Dear, excited and happy. Then Mr. Glover spoke with her and confirmed what Willie had told her. He further stated that he wanted to send the contract in the mail so that she and Daddy could look it over and then sign it if they approved. Mother told Mr. Glover to send it. Then Willie said, "Sign it when you get it and return it."

After Mother Dear had finished the phone conversation, she told me what she had been told and said to me, "I want you to look it over when it comes." I was happy too! I told her I would. The contract arrived shortly after, just as they had said it would. Mother Dear read it but said she didn't know if it should be signed or not. She wanted me to read it because I understood contracts better than the other members of the family. She gave it to me and asked me to read it. I did and explained the terms to her. Then she asked me if it was a good contract. I told her that it wasn't the best contract, but it was a good one. Then I continued, "You can take it to the lawyer and let him advise you if you wish, but it is a good contract." After taking it to the attorney, they were advised by the lawyer and he concluded that it was a good contract. So it was signed and sent back to New York. Mr. Glover took the master to the record plant and it was pressed. That made all of us happy to know that Willie would have a new record on the market by a new record company, King Records, in a few days. We already knew other artists who were signed to King Records.

So that was the record deal. But he wasn't finished just yet. He had to be signed with an agent. The agent, which is known as the booking agent, books all your dates where you will be performing. When and where, and

My Life and Experiences in the Entertainment World

for what amount of money. Well, that's a story within itself. For that, Willie visited the officers of Universal Attractions in New York City. Willie's personal agent who would work with him out of that office and would be responsible for his dates, was Ben Bart. After Ben saw that Willie had a new record on the market, he quickly wanted to sign him up to do dates. Willie told him to send the contract to his parents and they would sign it. Ben did send the contract, which was then signed and returned to him in New York. With that, Willie was in and all set to go on dates wherever they would lead him. He was booked all over the world!

All he had to do now was to wait for a few days until the record would be released and the dates would be lined up for him to go on the road again, this time with a national record release. But before the release, he was able to do a few gigs around New York and pick up a little much needed cash. Some of the popular places he played then were Club Shalamar, The Baby Grand Club, and the famous Smalls Paradise Club. By that time the new record had been shipped to radio disc jockeys across the country and shipments were being made to distributors too. I personally made a check at our distributor in Detroit to see if it had arrived here and I found that it had. The record company gave the release date to Willie so that he could let his promoters, as well as his audiences, know when the record would be in stores.

Ben Bart in the agent's office had already been successful in getting some dates for Willie. So it was time for him to see what was to be. In those early days of that new record, he was teamed with Hal Singer and his band. The office sent him down in the South to do a southern tour first. The tour went well, also, his record took off and eventually Willie had his first major hit in his first release on King Records. The tour later brought him home to do his first performance before his hometown audience. That was in the fall of the year. He was booked into the Mirrow Ballroom first. We were witnessing Willie's prediction which had come true. He had said sometime in the past that when he returned home, he would have a hit record. That he did indeed!

The record company wanted Willie to keep a hot record on the market. So he was called into the studio to cut his second record for his next release. The song Henry Glover had for him to record was, "I'm Sticking with You Baby," which was the "A" side. Again, Willie supplied the "B" side with a tune he had written titled, "Are You Ever Coming Back to Me?" The record was released at the time they had it scheduled to be released. The release helped to keep him hot on the road playing to big crowds.

Willie was not just another singer or performer, he was a very true, smooth, lyrical, distinguished singer. His style was all his own and very recognizable. There was no other like him. You could characterize his singing and performing as resolute. He was always determined to get the audience in his corner, as if to say, "I'm singing to you. This is your story and mine." Moreover, he was a very magnetic singer and performer in that he could

Mertis John

draw you to him. All this he did very well and it was all a part of his natural expression. I have seen many performers grab the microphone and play with it and play along with the audience. With it as if to throw it at them, but then catching it in time to draw it back in. I've seen performers such as James Brown, Jackie Wilson, and of course others do this. I'm not aiming to take anything away from these fine performers, I admire them both greatly. What I'm saying here is that I've seen performers on stage since the 1940s and I did not see any of them use the microphone in that manner until Willie started doing it on stage early in his career. What I'm saying is that this was an original thing of Willie's. Many others saw him do it, they used it, and it caught on. Willie was also one of the largest drawing cards in the R&B field in the 1950s and 1960s. During that time, 1956 and 1957, Willie was booked into the hottest club in Inkster, Michigan, Club Vogue, every chance that he would be available. For every date, the club would be filled to capacity for each performance. All the shows were hot. The opening act was Bobby Lewis. The house band for the club was the Cooking Band of Rip Reynolds. No band in the area could cook better than his could.

After I returned home from military service, I lived with Mable in her home on two occasions, before I was married. I first lived with her in Detroit after coming home, when she was no longer with her husband. They were subsequently divorced. Now later, she was married to the Reverend John Samuels. His work took him to Chicago so Mable and the children moved with him from Detroit to Chicago to make that their home. Still later, I went to Chicago to join Mable and travel with her on the road, which is the second time that I lived with her.

I must add, I really enjoyed being with my brother-in-law, John, especially during the time they were living in Chicago. I lived there in their home for one year. John was a great husband according to Mable, and I know he was also a great brother-in-law. He has passed on now and I do miss him. I will always remember him.

Chapter Ten

One of Willie's longtime ambitions was to purchase a home for Mother Dear. He had made a promise to her that after making enough money he would. Willie felt at this point, it was the time to do so. The next time he talked to her, he told her to start looking for the house she wanted him to buy for her. After looking at several homes, she decided on one she had found in the Russell Woods section of the city. Then Willie told her, before she stopped looking to make sure that this is the house you would be satisfied with. She said she was sure she would be satisfied with the choice she had made.

Before the deal was approved on the home, Willie had gotten another recording date. This would be his third recording session since signing with King Records. This one would also be different for me. I had written a song titled, "I Need Your Love So Bad." Willie wanted to record it in this session and that was fine with me. At the session, the song was presented. When Henry Glover heard it, he liked it. In fact, he liked it well enough to record it and make it the "A" side of the next release which would be the third release on King Records for Willie. So I was about to have my first song recorded and released. Now that was not the first song that I had written, but it was the right song to use at that point in time. After it's release, the record took off and became a big hit for Willie and for me. Little did I know at that time that the record would go on to be Willie's biggest hit up to that time.

Also, since that initial recording of the song, it has since been recorded about thirty-five times. The first person to cover "I Need Your Love So Bad" was Dakota Staton. Among others who have recorded the song are B. B. King and Little Milton. It has also been used on movie sound tracks.

Mertis John

It has been recorded worldwide. But first, let me not forget the record which became a huge hit for Willie during that time, "Home at Last."

After "I Need Your Love So Bad" moved up the charts and it was time for the next session, Willie and I went into the studio once more. The number one song on the list to be recorded in this session was "Fever." The Artist and Repertoire director and producer, Henry Glover, gave the song to Willie. We went over it in the studio for a while. Willie didn't like the song. Then he asked me, "Mert, do you like this song?"

I said, "No."

Then Henry said, "I want you to learn this song and do it first. If you don't do this one you can't do anything else you want to do." Then he told me to take Willie back to the hotel and make sure Willie learned this song. He was going to record it tomorrow night. We went back to the hotel. Willie still didn't want to do the song. I told him we had to learn it because it's this one or nothing. Willie and I both got on it. He learned the song that night and early the next day. I called Henry and asked what time did he want us at the studio. The first thing he asked was, "Did Willie learn that song?"

I told him, "Yes." Then he told me what time to come to the studio, and added, make sure Willie is here on time.

We went to the studio at the scheduled time. At session time, "Fever" was run down and then recorded. After being released, "Fever" climbed the charts very rapidly. It was being played everywhere. It proved to be Willie's biggest and most successful recording yet. It was the number one R&B record in the year of 1956. Even though no strings were used on this recording, the record was covered many times. Peggie Lee was the first to cover it and it proved to be a big hit for her also. Madonna recorded it some four or five years ago. After "Fever's" release, both Willie and I were very thankful that Henry demanded that Willie record it first.

After "Need Your Love So Bad," became a hit, I wanted to see strings used on Willie's future recordings. So at the next session I spoke with Henry Glover, the head of the A&R department, about it. I told him I felt that Willie's records should be given a sound that was more mellow and sweet. He in turn, told me to speak with Mr. Sid Nathan. I got to Mr. Nathan when I could and told him how I felt strings should be added to Willie's arrangements. I added, if they are used it would enhance the sound and give him a wider listening audience. Mr. Nathan said no strings would sell any more records than we would sell without them. The public would like it as is and buy it. I told him again, I think it would increase sales. Again, he said no it would not. Knowing all the time I was right, but I only said, "Okay Mr. Nathan." Then I went back into the studio.

That was in 1956. It was in early 1959, January I believe, when I heard Brook Benton's first big hit, "It's Just a Matter of Time." We all watched it climb the charts. Everybody started talking about it and how the strings made it sound so much better, with a fuller, richer sound. At our next

My Life and Experiences in the Entertainment World

recording session, Mr. Nathan didn't hesitate to say to Henry, "Yes, you can add a string arrangement to the session."

I was happy, but not nearly as happy as I would have been had Mr. Nathan given his okay on the use of strings back in 1956. It was something that I had envisioned. I wanted to be the first to use them on R&B records. When he didn't, it made me disappointed. With Brook's recordings, it started a trend that has continued even with today's recordings.

A little time later, Mother Dear and Daddy moved into the new home in Russell Woods. The children who were still living with them, Mildred, Delores, Raymond, and Toronto, also moved into the new home.

By this time, Willie was being labeled as a recording star and he was actually dominating the crowds on some shows where he wasn't getting top billing. But with his family, he would say he hadn't done anything. "Until I get Mother Dear in that house she wants to move into." After they had made the move into the new home, Willie was very happy, relieved, and tremendously proud of his accomplishments. You could even see the happiness on his face.

The Apollo Theatre in New York City was the place to play. In the business, until you played the Apollo in New York, you had not made it. Willie was booked into the Apollo for the first time, headlining the show. Before the show opened, Willie called Mother Dear and reminded her that he was opening at the Apollo that night. He said that he was nervous. Mother Dear asked why. He said, "This is the Apollo. Here either you make it or you're out."

She said, "Willie, you're going to make it."

Then Willie said, "Pray for me, Mother Dear."

Mother Dear immediately went into prayer. Afterwards she called his attention to something she had told us years before and it's this, "You will be playing before big crowds. Remember you must make Mother proud. Everything will be all right." She told him to call her after the show and let her know how everything had gone. He wanted this to be his best show ever. He said that he wanted to give the audience something that they had never seen and he hoped they would like it. When he called back, he told us the show went great. The audience really loved it. We were all proud and happy for him.

Willie's ambition was to perform before all audiences, to record songs that would catch everyone's ear, and to gain respect from the total listening audience. For that, he said, "I have to make them all like me."

It was about this time that he asked me to join him on the road so I certainly did, very shortly after. I flew to Dallas to meet him. We had a Texas tour of one-nighters lined up which would take at least one month to complete. Texas is a very large state and the tour took us up and down, and across it as well. I remember one of our promoters in Texas was the well respected Mr. Howard Lewis. As I recollect, the entire tour was a tour of one-nighters. In other words, you find yourself in a different city each night until you complete the tour. On this tour, some of the popular places in Texas we played were Dallas, Sherman, Ft. Worth, Arlington, Irving, Longview, Tyler, Marshall, Waco, Temple, Austin, San Antonio, Floresville, Corpus Christi, Greenville, Gainesville, Wichita Falls, Beaumont, Port Arthur, La Marque, Galveston, Kilgore, Lubbock, Houston, Wharton, Kingsville, McAllen, and Brownsville. Then we crossed over into Mexico and played Juarez, Sonora, Hermosillo, Monterey, Tampico, Saltillo, etc.

While doing this Texas tour, our car broke down in some county town between Houston and Dallas. I don't remember the name of the place, but I'll never forget how prejudiced the White people were. We stopped for food early that morning. White people didn't want to wait on us. We found out that we had to go around to the back of the place to order what we wanted and even at that, they would only serve us carry-out orders. Then we went to the bus station to get a cab and we were told that we had to wait for a Black cab driver. We needed a cab to take us to find a Black mechanic to repair the car. We finally were able to get a Black cab driver to go and find a Black mechanic. The mechanic took us to his home where we would be able to eat and relax until he repaired whatever was wrong with the car. Then he brought the car to us.

There was a lady in the house who I believe was his mother. She prepared a nice breakfast for us then we relaxed and waited until our car was ready. There was no water in the house and there was no toilet. So here was a new experience for us. There was a water source available only by a water pump on the back porch. The only way to get water was to pour water into it in order to get water out by pumping. This is what the lady did to get water. The water, however, was very cool to drink. The toilet was still another story. The toilet was a very small wooden house which sat about one hundred fifty feet or so from the house in the back. They called it an outhouse. You had to go out to it when you needed to be relieved. The lady was very friendly and cordial. We appreciated that, but they were also a long way from being up-to-date, in reference to sanitation and convenience.

Our car was finally ready. Our driver, John D. Jones came and picked us up and again, we were on our way to Dallas. This tour ended in Dallas. We were scheduled to be in Washington, D.C., the next day, to get ready for our next tour which would be with a package show. The car took us to Love Field, the airport in Dallas, where we flew on to Washington, D.C. We left Dallas and arrived in Washington on Saturday. That was the day I met the one, the only, Little Richard. He went on to become world famous. We were at our hotel and Willie told me, "Mert, come on go with me. I want you to meet someone." So we walked to his room. Someone let us in. Willie said, "This is who I want you to meet. This is Little Richard." Then Richard and I introduced ourselves. He happened to be getting his hair done at the time we met. Later at the rehearsal, I was able to meet all the other performers and band members who we would be working with on this tour. The performers aside from Little Richard and Little Willie John

My Life and Experiences in the Entertainment World

included Ruth Brown and Fats Domino. The singing groups included The Clovers, The Cadillacs, The Turbans, The Sweethearts, two lovely ladies called Dottie and Millie, Al Jackson and his Fat Man Quartet, and Joe Medlin. The band who backed everyone up on the show was Choker Campbell and his big band.

Our booking office had put together a very accommodating group of entertainers and musicians. There were sold-out crowds in every city which we played on this tour. All the artists were ready to give their best and please each and every audience who came to see the shows in every city. They got what they came for and they were pleased in every city.

I personally enjoyed each city on this tour immensely. The only negative experiences we had were some prejudice situations in the South when we had to stop for food or to use the restrooms. We had two buses on this tour, one for the band and the other for the other artists. A representative from the booking office traveled with us. The representative was White, of course. He would order our food. The bus drivers would always find parking places in the rear of the restaurants. After we would get our food, the drivers would continue on to our destination. Our representative would make sure we all got to our rooms at the hotels. He would also see that we all got paid.

The following is a list of the dates we did on this tour. Note that there were thirty-six dates on this tour and they were all one-nighters. Actually, you could make the greatest amount of money doing one-nighters.

PROPOSED PROSPECTIVE ITINERARY – RHYTHM & BLUES of 1956

DATE		TOWN	PLACE
APRIL	1	Richmond, Va.	The Mosque
	2	Charlotte, N. C.	Armory
	3	Winston Salem, N. C.	Mem. Coll.
	4	Upper Darby, Pa. (Phila.)	Tower Theatre
	5	Baltimore, Md.	Coliseum
	6	Newark, N. J.	Mosque Audit.
	7	Norfolk, Va.	Audit.
	8	Wash. D. C.	Audit.
	9	Saratoga Springs, N. Y.	Convention Hall
	10	Toronto, Canada	Mutual Arena
	11	Pittsburgh, Pa.	Syria Mosque
	12	Buffalo	Memorial Arena
	13	Columbus, Ohio	Vet. Mem. Audit.
	14	Indianapolis, Ind.	Tomlinson Hall
	15	Kansas City, Mo.	Music Hall
	16	Tulsa, Okla.	Theatre Audit.

Mertis John

	17	Okla, City, Okla.	Auditorium
	18	Houston, Texas	Auditorium
	19	Ft. Worth, Texas	Will Rogers Audit.
	20	Dallas, Texas	Sportorium
	21	Austin, Texas	Auditorium
	22	New Orleans, La.	Field House Lyola Univ.
	23	Memphis, Tenn.	Hippodrome Ballroom
	24	Nashville, Tenn.	A & I College Gym
	25	Chattanooga, Tenn.	Auditorium
	26	Atlanta, Ga.	Auditorium
	27	Raleigh, N. C.	Auditorium
	28	Charleston, S. C.	County Hall
	29	Augusta, Ga.	Bell Audit.
	30	Kingston, N. C.	Warehouse
May	1	Knoxville, Tenn.	Chillhowee Pk.
	2	Greenville, S. C.	Textile Hall
	3	Fayettville, N. C.	Breece's Landing
	4	Roanoke, Va.	Auditorium
	5	Columbia, S. C.	Auditorium
	6	Birmingham, Ala.	Auditorium

NOTE: Correct Place April 1st – Correct Town & Place April 9th and 23rd.

There will be a rehearsal at TURNER'S ARENA, 1341 "W" St., N.W., Washington, D. C. at 2:30 P.M. on Saturday, March 31st.

Two buses will leave from in front of the THRESA HOTEL, 125th St. and 7th Ave., N.Y.C. at 8:30 A.M. Saturday, March 31st, arriving in Washington in time for the 2:30 rehearsal.

We had a lot of fun riding the bus from city to city and being able to talk with the various entertainers who were a part of the show. Willie was the youngest member of the show. He kept his usual thing going on the bus, playing a lot and talking a lot. He did most of his playing on this tour with Little Richard, joking a lot. He did most of his serious talking to Ruth Brown. She and Fats Domino had more show business experience than the other artists on the show at that time.

While we were in Portsmouth, Virginia, I had a chance to visit Ruth Brown's home and to meet some of her family members. That was fun. I also remember that she was funding one relative's tuition while attending school away from home.

This was not however, the end of the tour. We had still a long way to go. Rather, it was because we happened to be in the vicinity of her home at that time that we stopped. So the tour rolled on. After finishing this tour,

My Life and Experiences in the Entertainment World

there was another ready to start. So goes the world of entertainment. But I did enjoy it. Yes, I did. We did tour after tour all of that year which was 1956. In 1957, something else happened for me. As a matter of fact, it happened for Willie also.

In1957, I got married. As a matter of fact, Willie and I were married a week or two apart. We both married in June. Willie was married to the Miss Darlynn Bonner of Philadelphia, Pennsylvania. This marriage produced two wonderful sons, William Kevin and Daryl Keith. After growing up and following in the footsteps of their dad, they subsequently became involved in show business also. They made recordings and went on to work with Stevie Wonder.

Their mother Darlynn had been a member of the famous Hortense Allen Dance Group before her marriage to Willie. Willie and Darlynn were married in the home which he had purchased for Mother Dear. The marriage meant that he had the dream of a house to fulfill with his wife also.

Even though Willie was from Detroit and Darlynn was from Philadelphia, when it came to selecting an area where they wanted their home to be as husband and wife, they settled on Florida. They selected a fabulous home in Miami which Willie purchased for her and their family. Later, she, Willie, and their sons lived in the home. Sometime later after Willie had passed away, Darlynn and the boys came back to Detroit to be near the John Family.

Aside from being talented, Willie was very free with his money. It was easy come, easy go with him. When he would come home off the road, he would drive through old familiar neighborhoods with money in his pocket and when he saw old friends or acquaintances, he would stop them and ask if they needed any money. Most often they would say yes. Then he would give them money. When he would walk into bars or night clubs, he would often set up the house.

Even when he was away from home, he would set up bars. Many people would ask for money on the street and other places as well, and he would give money to them. Some people knew that he was very generous with his money; they would come to the stage door to ask him for money. He would sometimes give money to them. The times when I heard them ask for money, I would hear a many sad story.

When we were in the car, he made sure there was always a Bible in the car at all times. If we were traveling from one city to another, he would always ask me if I had prayed. He knew that I always did. If I said, "Yes," then he would say, "Then everything is all right." If I said I had not he would say, "Go ahead and pray." He always felt at ease after I had prayed.

I married Essie Wincher. Our marriage produced a wonderful son, Darryl Emmanuel, who is a fine son. Although he didn't pursue the dream I had intended for him, he did pursue his own dream. Since I'm a songwriter I wanted to teach him to become the same. I dreamed that someday we would become a writing team. He studied the piano from age five to

Mertis John

age twelve. That however, did not make him grasp the desire to stay with music. At age twelve, he told me he had a love for figures. Subsequently, he went on to graduate from high school at age sixteen, then went on to college to receive his degree in business. He did show some skill and love in writing poetry early in life when I introduced poetry writing to him. He did follow me in that regard. I'm proud of you son. You pursued your dream!

The following poem is dedicated to my son, Darryl:

Also, in 1957, I did not go on the road. Instead, I enrolled in the Detroit Conservatory of Music where I studied the piano. This continued through 1958. I wrote quite a number of songs during those two years. Several of the songs were written for Willie. One of which was, "You Hurt Me," which was subsequently recorded by him.

In early 1959, I rejoined Willie on the road. I don't remember the exact place where we met up, but I do remember that it was on the east coast and that we eventually toured all over the country. We did the Howard Theatre in the city of Washington, D.C.; played the Royal Theatre in Baltimore; played other places in Maryland; played Richmond, Virginia; and in New York City it was the Apollo Theatre and the Rockland Palace. While we were in New York City, a recording session was scheduled to be done at Bell Sound Studio, so we were in the studio for about five days. From that session came "Let Them Talk," "Leave My Kitten Alone," and "I Love You Because You Are," or "Let Nobody Love You." It was a very good session. The recordings were done with a big band and strings.

After the session was finished, we resumed doing the travel show dates. Houston, Texas was calling. While there, we ran into singer Big Momma Thornton. We had lots of fun together. She's the one who had written and recorded, "Hound Dog." She wrote and recorded it first on the Duke record label, later Elvis Presley recorded it and it became a huge hit. We then moved on to Birmingham and Selma, Alabama; Atlanta, Georgia; Nashville and Memphis, Tennessee; then on to Cleveland, Ohio; Pittsburgh, Pennsylvania; Buffalo, New York; Saratoga Springs, New York; Newark, New Jersey; New Haven and Hartford, Connecticut; Boston and Holyoke, Massachusetts; Rochester, New York; Upper Darby, Pennsylvania; Scranton, Pennsylvania; Louisville and Lexington, Kentucky; Charleston, West Virginia; and Hampton, Virginia.

While traveling during this same time through the South, we stopped in Greensboro, North Carolina at the urging of Clarence Avant, Willie's Road Manager. Either he or a member of his family had attended North Carolina A&T State University, located there in Greensboro, North Carolina. He said that we could spend the night on the campus in the dormitory rather than look for a hotel or a rooming house. Remember, in those days it was not always easy for Black people to acquire hotel space in a good hotel or motel. Many times we had to secure rooms at a rooming

A Son of Whom I'm Proud

(Dedicated To My Son Darryl)

I still remember that very special day
It was January 25, a happy and joyous day
We were very excited, but prepared for this event
Words can hardly describe what having you meant

Your head firm and round, your eyes like a shining light
Whenever we looked at you, you smiled with much delight
When it was time for you to crawl, you didn't crawl at all
Instead you scooted around, then pulled up and tried to walk

Oh, what a day it was when you said your first words. . . "DA DA, DA DA"
That made me feel very proud, it made me feel that you cared
Soon we will travel here and there
On open road and sometimes by air

It was a thrill to watch you grow
What would you become in life
I really didn't know
Musician, Doctor, Lawyer all would be fine

One day I asked out of curiosity,
"Tell me, what are you going to be?" you replied,
"I like figures, can't you see?
Working with Math satisfies me."

Would you believe, just like he said,
He stayed with that Math, Geometry, and Trigonometry
He kept reaching high, knowing someday he would be
A well-learned scholar with a well-earned degree.

Copyright 1996
By Mertis John

Mertis John

house which was run by a Black person. So Clarence had a good idea in mind, and we took him up on it. After all, he was the road manager. He knew some of the faculty members at the school and was sure that we could spend the night there.

Clarence directed us there and just like he had said, they accepted us with open arms. We were given rooms in one of the dormitories. The next morning we had a tasty breakfast in the cafeteria. While we were there, we spoke with many students which included those students who had intended sit-ins in hopes of desegregating first the lunch counters at Woolworth's store, and later other places of business that discriminated against Black people. We wished them God's speed. As we all know now, they were successful in their very courageous endeavor. Because of them and others who followed them in their efforts to change the consciousness of this nation, we now are able to live a fuller life. I commend them and realize we owe them much. In retrospect, that was a struggle which should never had to be experienced. Because five years earlier, on May 17, 1954, the United States Supreme Court, in the landmark Brown vs. The Board of Education decision, rules unanimously that racial segregation in public schools was unconstitutional. The decision which was read by Chief Justice Earl Warren, said that the "Separate-But-Equal" doctrine enunciated by the Supreme Court in 1896 had "no place" in public education. It continued, "Separate educational facilities are inherently unequal," the ruling affected 17 states which had compulsory public school segregation and four which permitted school segregation. Sixteen states prohibited school segregation and eleven had no laws regulating it at all. We moved on from Greensboro, North Carolina and North Carolina A&T State University, but I have never forgotten the eagerness, confidence, determination, and yes, faith those students displayed to us in what they were attempting to accomplish. Their efforts paid off not only for them, but for all of us.

We traveled to Charlotte, North Carolina; Atlanta and Columbus, Georgia; Montgomery, Birmingham and Huntsville, Alabama; Chattanooga, Knoxville, Nashville, and Memphis, Tennessee; Oklahoma City and Tulsa, Oklahoma; Wichita and Topeka, Kansas; St. Louis, Missouri; Cedar Rapids, Iowa; Milwaukee and Madison, Wisconsin; Waterloo and Des Moines, Iowa; Omaha and Lincoln, Nebraska; Cheyenne, Wyoming; Denver, Colorado Springs and Pueblo, Colorado; Santa Fe and Albuquerque, New Mexico; and Tucson and Phoenix, Arizona.

Chapter Eleven

Louis Jordan was a very popular saxophonist and band leader who also sung during the 1940s. He later moved to Phoenix, Arizona, because the weather there was more conducive to his health. Aside from his home there where he lived, he also had another home directly across the street. It was used for a guest home for entertainers when they came to town. Each time we were in Phoenix, we would stay at his guest house. We had a wonderful time each time we visited. Louis kept you laughing when he was off stage, as well as when he was on stage. I always enjoyed being around him. Louis was a very wonderful fellow. He was a fine musician, as well as a natural comedian. Then we traveled to California to play San Diego to Los Angeles, and all the major places, as well as many smaller places in between. From the south up the coast, places that are too numerous to mention.

We then continued up the Pacific Coast into Eugene, Salem, and of course Portland, Oregon. Then on to Tacoma, Spokane, Seattle and Olympia, Washington. After playing that area, we crossed over into the Canadian Northwest where we were in Vancouver, British Columbia. Usually then, after we had completed a tour of the country, the agent would have dates lined up for you to complete the circuit once more. This is what happened then.

The next time we played California the Great Count Basie and his big wonderful band were also playing through California. We really had a wonderful time on this tour. I have always admired the big band sound including of course Basie's sound. I had a chance to be around him for a good period of time and we talked a lot. We also had been doing engagements at

Mertis John

the same time through Texas and on the East Coast. Count Basie was one of the people in the entertainment industry that I most admired. I'm grateful to God for having the chance to tell him so while he was still alive.

Now when we would run into each other on the road, we would always go to each other's performances. On his shows he would call Willie up to the stage to sing a couple of songs. I would always enjoy hearing Willie sing with Count's big band just as I did this time in San Francisco at the Fisherman's Wharf. I can't forget too, that the great Joe Williams was the vocalist for his band then. We all had happy times together. The drummer for the band in those days was Sonny Payne. We had fun together also. He was a good drummer, but I also like the way he would spin his sticks around while he played. I would tell him how I liked to see and hear him play and that he was very cool playing the drums. We would have a big laugh about it and then he would thank me.

I must mention something terribly frightening that happened during our stay in San Francisco on that last trip. It wasn't at all funny, but the incident made us thank God a lot more. Willie was a smoker. The last thing he would do at night before going to bed was smoke a cigarette. He would sit on or near the bed for the last smoke of the day. Sometimes he would fall asleep while smoking. I would awake him many times but this particular time I didn't catch him smoking in bed. We slept together many times on the road.

It was a blessing for us that night when our driver smelled smoke, came to the door and saw smoke coming from the room. He awakened us and we saw that the room was full of smoke. We then discovered that the mattress we were sleeping on was on fire. Willie had fallen asleep while smoking. The cigarette had ignited the mattress. Good thing we had not been burned! We got out of bed, picked up whatever we could find that would hold water, filled it, and poured it on the burning mattress. We continued this until we thought it had all been put out. We couldn't get back in bed, but we did fall asleep.

Sometime later that night we began to smell smoke once more. Much to our surprise, the mattress was burning again. We didn't know how difficult it is to put out a fire in a burning mattress. We didn't know when firemen found burning mattresses in buildings, they throw them out for the safety of the building then deal with them outside of the building. A mattress fire can fool you, especially when you are not familiar in dealing with them. In the end, we did learn a lesson from that experience. I'll tell you this…that was a night that I will never forget for as long as I live. I thank God, He saved our lives and no harm came to us.

There was one final chapter to this experience. The cost of all the damage that was incurred had to be taken care of before we could check out of the hotel. So the hotel came up with a figure and gave it to Willie and he paid that sum to the hotel. We then were able to check out of the hotel and continue on to the next engagement.

My Life and Experiences in the Entertainment World

Earlier in Chapter Ten, I spoke of the time that my brother, Willie, his Road Manager Clarence Avant, and I stayed overnight on the campus of North Carolina A&T. We visited many college campuses. I made it a point to visit every predominantly Black college possible during the times that I was on tour. I wanted to meet students, talk with them, and hear how they compared their schools to those that are larger and well known. In doing so, I learned a great deal about how they are run and what types of basic instructions students receive.

Here is a list of some of the colleges that I visited: Texas Southern University, Fisk University, Tennessee State A&I, Meharry Medical College, Dillard University, Morehouse College, Central State University, Clark College, Florida A&M University, Hampton University, Howard University, Southern University A&M College, Grambling State University, Tuskegee University, Philander Smith College, Spelman College, Albany State University, and Prairie View A&M University.

After learning about the above schools and those others belonging to be listed, such as Martin Luther King, Jr.; Barbara Jordan; and Wilma Rudolph, because they are all institutions caring about the task of providing every young person who wishes a higher education to make it possible and to prepare them for today's world, as well as tomorrow's world. Seeing the dedication of the faculty members to motivate and educate each student to perform to their highest potential has made my number one charity organization the United Negro College Fund.

I came home off the road with Willie in November, 1960 because my wife and I were expecting our first child around Christmas. To our surprise, we didn't have a Christmas baby as we had expected. The child was not born until one month later and in a new year. I was wishing for a girl. She was wishing for a boy. I didn't get my wish, however on January 25th of the next year, we were presented the gift of a baby boy. I was, however, just as proud of him as I would have been had the bundle of joy been a girl. I stayed home to be with the new addition to the family and to help care for him for nine months. It was a good thing that I did because the baby was not a night sleeper. He slept during the day and kept me up each night. I had learned how to care for him and how to feed him which I did. I got most of my sleep during the day. After a short while, I became familiar with the routine that I had to maintain, and at the same time, I was having lots of fun with my son.

After that period ended, I prepared to go to Chicago to be with my sister Mable. The next tour for her was being lined up and she had asked me if I would accompany her on the tour. Of course, I told her that I would, so I went to Chicago. While I was there, before the tour was to start, I would hang out at a certain barber shop. It was Jimmy's Barber Shop located on 63rd Street at South Parkway. South Parkway was later named Martin Luther King Drive. Jimmy was a very nice older, well informed barber. We eventually became good friends. He invited me to his home and I accepted

Mertis John

the invitation. We also attended baseball games together at Comiskey Park when the Chicago White Sox were playing at home. He had other barbers in the shop working for him also. He, along with two of them began to tell me that I should become a barber. I asked them how could I become a barber when I'm in music and traveling all over. They told me that I could be a barber and continue to do what I was doing. They said, "You work as a barber when you want to. Otherwise, do what else you like to do." I listened to them. They further asked me to promise them that when I returned home I would check out a barber college and enroll.

One of my barbers, as a young boy growing up, was the father of two of my school mates, John Livingston and his brother Billy Livingston. John and I were classmates. They both became barbers through their father. John, who was the oldest, has even cut my hair. Even seeing this did not make me aspire to become a barber. I was already set, I felt. Their shop was located on Davison Avenue, west of Dequindre. The shop was always busy with patrons. A little later in the book, I will talk about how the shop in Chicago affected my life later on.

I began to accompany my sister Mable on tour. She recorded for Tamla/Motown Records. She had scored with such tunes as, "Who Wouldn't Love a Man Like That," b/w "You Made a Fool Out of Me," which was her first release on Motown's Tamla label. We hit the road and traveled to our first stop which was Indianapolis to play the famous Pink Poodle Club. Also on that bill was the very funny Pigmeat Markham, a comedian. From there we went to Evansville, Memphis, and to Chattanooga, Tennessee. Then on to the New Era Club in Nashville, Tennessee; Huntsville and Birmingham, Alabama; Atlanta, Georgia; and Tampa, Florida. We came back home to the Graystone Ballroom and the Gold Coast Theatre, then up to Flint at the MIA Auditorium. Jackie Wilson, The Five Royals, and Walter Jackson were also on this bill. Early on, Mable had played the famous Flame Show on John R. She was on the bill then with the late great Billie Holiday and the one and only Maurice King and his band at the Flame. There was also a dancer on the bill at that time, but I don't recall her name.

Professionally and musically, I first ran into Berry Gordy at a music publishing and songwriting office on Alexandrine, 28 W. Alexandrine to be exact. He was writing for a few people at the time and soon he made the hit scene by writing some tunes for Jackie Wilson. Other music people whom I met there were Billy Davis and Alonso Tucker. I was also writing then for some singers, but most of my writing was for my brother, Willie. I had already had my first hit, "Need Your Love So Bad," recorded by Willie. Pearl Music Publishing Company was a part of the operations there also. Al Green (not the singer) who owned the Flame Show Bar and also managed some singers there. My brother's personal manager, Harry Balk also had an office there. Eventually I met Nat Tarnopol, who was to become

My Life and Experiences in the Entertainment World

Jackie Wilson's personal manager. I wrote out of that office for a short time, working with Alonso Tucker.

After Berry moved to 2648 West Grand Boulevard and started Hitsville USA, I worked there for a while. I sometimes drove Berry to radio stations to promote his records when he didn't have a car. This is how I met Janie Bradford, a secretary who worked in the publishing department; Holland, Dozier, and Holland, who were to become world renown writers and producers, and William Mickey Stevenson, who was the director of Artist and Repertoire. Janie and my family have been close friends since those days. We still do things together and support each other. Berry's wife at that time, Raynoma (we call her Ray) and I already had known each other a long time. She was a friend of the family so we didn't have to get acquainted. She headed the Publishing Office along with her brother Mike Ossman. Smokey Robinson and the Miracles were there, the Temptations, and others. Marvin Gaye was also there and other musicians such as James Jemerson, Joseph Hunter, Bennie Benjamin, and Popcorn Wylie to name a few.

So I did some writing for her. I wrote "We Belong Together" and "Give My Thanks to You" for her. I also worked with William Stevenson. Berry invited me to stay around the Motown Studio and continue writing songs for Motown, but I was already writing for Willie and King Records. I already had several hits and I was experiencing a degree of success there also. Thinking it over, I felt it would be best for me to stay with King Records. So that's what I decided to do.

Shortly afterwards, my friend Joseph Hunter, who was also a musician at Motown, was playing a weekly gig in Ecorse, Michigan at Chappie's Lounge. The singer on the show was Kim Weston. This was just before she was signed by Motown Records. Joe would let me do guest solos on the show, although I was not booked into the club.

I Met Many Famous People

Being in business has afforded me the marvelous opportunity to meet many famous people. It was always a thrill meeting and being with people who are well-known, but if you are not a songwriter (as I am), there is another wonderful thrill that you will never experience: The thrill of someone using your material, then hearing it played on the airwaves. It is a thrill for me to write a song, take it to the recording studio and present it, then teach it to an artist and have them record it. But the greatest thrill of all comes later when you hear your music being played on the radio and television. That's a feeling so great it's almost indescribable. I'll never forget when I heard my first song being played on the airways. That was a moment that I will savor for the rest of my life.

I estimate that Joe Louis and Sugar Ray Robinson were two of the very best fighters that ever lived. I always wanted to meet both of them not knowing or even believing that I would ever have the opportunity. Joe Louis became the heavyweight champion of the world by knocking out

Mertis John

James J. Braddock in 1937 in Chicago. He went on to hold the championship longer than anyone else. He was one fighter who came to win and he was a real winner. I met him first in 1947. Sugar Ray Robinson was a sweet and smooth fighter, a finished boxer. He was the best fighter pound for pound. He beat Jake Lamotta to be crowned the Middleweight Champion of the World on February 26, 1943. He also held the Welterweight Championship title. The fight was held in Detroit at the Olympia Stadium. Later he fought for the Light Heavyweight Championship in temperatures of 100 degrees and was winning the fight until the heat not his opponent, caught up with him.

I became acquainted with Sugar Ray when my brother Willie introduced us while we were in New York in 1956. I found him to be a very open and friendly person. He owned businesses that took up a whole city block on Seventh Avenue in Harlem, New York. He owned restaurants, cleaners, and a barbershop. I spent several days in his company. He seemed to enjoy talking with me. I certainly enjoyed talking with him and being around him. He was a lot of fun and an inspiration to me.

In 1947, Jackie Robinson broke the color barrier in professional baseball when he was signed by the Brooklyn Dodgers. By doing so, he accepted a role so difficult that only a few people could have ever survived it successfully. Thank God he triumphed over prejudice and hate. By doing so, he opened up the doors of opportunity to countless Blacks. Thereafter, Black people were accepted to participate and to compete in all professional sports. I first saw Jackie when his first season with the Brooklyn Dodgers ended and he came to Detroit to play on his barnstorming tour. They played at Dequindre Park, the same park where I played baseball. I didn't meet him on that day, but I subsequently met him in 1956 in Baltimore when we were playing at the Royal Theatre.

Jackie played as a member of the Brooklyn Dodgers from 1947–1955. In 1956, he was traded to the crosstown rival team the New York giants. However, Jackie didn't accept the trade. Instead, he retired from baseball. I had hoped that he would extend his career by accepting the trade and playing for another four years or so, but that was not his wish.

On the baseball field, Robinson was a very swift and sure-handed infielder who batted .387 for the Kansas City Monarchs of the Negro American League in 1945. Still the White press was not impressed with his major league potential. However, Robinson went on to lead the Dodgers to six pennants and one world championship during his ten-year career. He earned the National League's Most Valuable Player Award in 1949 and he entered the Hall of Fame in 1962.

On October 24, 1972, Jackie Robinson passed away.

In 1953 or 1954, the New York Giants were one of baseball's top teams, led by center fielder Willie Mays. After the season ended, the team traveled to Korea to spread good cheer to the military troops who were there. I was serving in Korea at that time. I met the team's manager who

My Life and Experiences in the Entertainment World

was Leo Durocher and Willie Mays. Leo was called "The Lip" and I found out why. He loved to talk and he talked a great deal, but I also found out the man had something to say. I enjoyed him. After I returned home, I saw a lot more of Willie. As we toured the country during the baseball season, we would go to games when we were in the same city. We also stayed at the same hotels in some cities. Willie like to call me "John John."

In the 1950s there was a popular White singer who was a balladeer; his name was Billy Farrow. I met him in Pittsburgh when he was splaying a club there around 1956. He had a mellow voice as I recall.

One of the best and most respected pianist from the 1940s to the 1970s was a man who hailed from Pittsburgh, Pennsylvania. He had a style all his own, playing popular standards with his melodic variations. He had a very gifted left hand which was as melodic as his right hand. That is what set him apart from other piano styles and made him so recognizable from all others. The person I'm speaking of is Errol Garner. I knew Errol; we were friends. He left us in 1977, but he had already made his indelible mark in the world of show business. His most famous recording was "Misty," and his most popular LP was *Concert By The Sea*.

One of the real crooners to come along in the 1950's was Johnny Mathis. When Johnny hit the scene, he gave us the best that San Francisco had to offer. But he wasn't just good for his native home of San Francisco, he was good for all of us. I spent time with him in the 1950s. I met Johnny in 1959 when he was playing the Latin Quarter in Philadelphia. My brother Willie, and I, along with his wife Darlynn, were at the club that night to see his performance. He gave an incredible performance which we thoroughly enjoyed! After the show, we went back stage to chat with him. We found a long line of young ladies waiting to see him and to get his autograph. Seeing him wasn't automatic. His manager, Helen Nogo, was there and made sure none of the ladies saw him until he was ready to accept them for autographs. We went in and he greeted Willie after he was announced. Willie introduced him to me, and we all chatted for a while. He said that he would be on the golf course at a certain time the following day. He invited us to join him there; we did. We spent that next day together, and it was really wonderful.

That same year, 1959, while working in the South and in the East, there were dates that we shared with Brooke Benton when he was also on the show with Willie. Brooke was a very smooth singer of R&B ballads. I loved his voice as well as his style and his choice of songs. He was also a songwriter, and he wrote his own songs. He wrote songs for some other singers as well. I enjoyed being around him.

I had heard so much talk about the person that I'm about to talk about now. Many things that I had heard about her weren't complimentary. Hearing those comments caused me to be reluctant to meet her. In my mind I really wanted to meet her, but at the same time I wanted our meeting to be pleasant and lasting. Well now I was about to meet her. In 1956,

Mertis John

Dinah Washington's name and style of singing had been established for years. She was one of our top-notch female entertainers. Her name was synonymous with such singers as Billie Holiday, Sarah Vaughn, and Ella Fitzgerald. She was known as the Queen of the Blues though she would quickly tell you, "I can sing anything, including ballads." She was right. Later in her career, she sang many ballads and handled them with the utmost professionalism and style. Dinah was working in a club in Philadelphia when Willie and I went to see her. He had met her sometime before, so we were ushered to her dressing room. "I want you to meet my brother Mertis," Willie said as we walked in, "This is my oldest brother."

She laughed and said, "Oh, I'm looking for a good man!"

Willie said, "He's a good man." We had a good laugh. I found her to be very friendly and open. We subsequently became friends. Some years later, she was married to Night Train Lane, a former Detroit Lion Player, and moved to my hometown, Detroit. She's now out of our sight, but not out of our minds. I was hurt and saddened when she left us so soon, at the height of her career. However, she is one person and entertainer that I will always remember.

The person I wish to talk about now is Sam Cooke. Sam had a "God given gift" of singing. Not all singers have the gift to sing, but Sam was one who had. He started using his gift at an early age, when he began singing in church. Even sometime later when he joined one of the premier gospel groups in the world, the Soul Stirrers, also known as the Highway QC's, he was a singer of only gospel. He always reminded me of my family. We, too, started out singing only gospel music. Sam was the son of a Baptist Minister. That is where he got his soulful feeling right there in the church.

I stated that Sam had a "God given gift" of singing. So, when he decided to make the move from singing gospel to singing secular music, he could handle any type of song with equal quality and finesse as he had always handled gospel. He demonstrated just that much versatility.

A singer with his gift did not need to use any gimmicks or tell any jokes as a performer. Sam did not. All he did was what he did best—walk out onto the stage and sing. He was one of the best in the business.

Sam was a friend of my family. He would come by my mother's home when he was in town. When he couldn't make it over, he would call. I remember the time just before he was shot and killed, around 1964 or 1965. Two or three weeks before, I began to think about Sam quite strongly every day. I could not get him off my mind. I had not seen, or heard from him for some time, so then I called Mother Dear because she would sometimes hear from him when I didn't. I called and asked had she seen or heard from him. She said, "No. Do you have anything to tell him?"

I told her, "No, nothing in particular. He's just been on my mind lately, every day." Then I told her if she saw or spoke with him before I did, please tell him to get in touch with me.

My Life and Experiences in the Entertainment World

Neither one of us knew then that we would never see Sam alive again. A very few days after our conversation, we all heard the news about his tragic death. Sam had been shot by a woman in a Los Angeles motel. I'll never believe the story which circulated around as the reason for his death.

The woman who shot him claimed her innocence. To my knowledge, nothing has happened to her in reference to paying for the crime and I often wondered why. In losing Sam, we lost a friend, a true singer and entertainer, and a very soulful person. Sam, you are definitely missed!

Between the years of 1959 to 1965, my younger brother Raymond had a yearning to burst onto the record scene as a hit maker. He worked some clubs in Detroit, one being the Chit Chat Lounge on 12th Street. He also had a part in the stage play, *Little Red*. He helped to produce a session for singer Big Mabelle in New York City. He has also worked at some clubs there and wrote songs. Once he was working on a song entitled, "In My Hands." He wrote the first two verses, then couldn't get the chorus. He then got on the phone and called me. "Mert," he said, "I'm writing a song but I can't come up with the chorus. Can you come up with one for this song?" I asked him to run down what he had so that I had something to work from. I came up with something that fit right in. I gave it to him and he said, "Oh yes...That's it!!! Then I proceeded to write the next verse. We then put it all together. Thus, we had the song, "In My Hands." Raymond possessed a good singing voice as well.

After my sister Mable left Motown Records and went to Stax Records, Raymond did some backup vocals on some of her records. In 1964, Mable, Raymond, and I traveled to Stax for a record session. In that session, I remember one song in particular where he did backup vocals. The song was, "Your Love Gets Bigger and Better."

Chapter Twelve

In 1962, after I had returned home, I kept my promise that I had made with Jimmy and two other barbers who worked for him in his Chicago shop. I enrolled in the Universal Barber College. I attended full-time so that I could learn the skills and the other formal training and knowledge that goes along with being a good barber. After successfully completing the course, I received my diploma. I then took the state examination and passed with flying colors.

I subsequently became the owner of my own barber shop, "Artistic Barber Shop." I made it just as I had promised. The building where the shop was located also had space for a store. I had wanted to own a record store for sometime now. The building was located at 5127–5129 Chene Street, a very busy street with lots of traffic and shoppers. In addition to the record line, I also sold record accessories such as needles, adapters, news magazines, papers, cigarettes, stockings, wigs, and cassette tape players once they hit the market. My son Darryl was a youngster then but he loved working in the record store. He learned how to take inventory and spent his working time between the store and the barber shop. I suppose working in the barber shop and record store helped to shape his future. He told me he liked working with figures. I operated the store for ten years. The barber shop is a different story; it lasted thirty-five years.

Working in the store was a family affair. In addition to my son Darryl and me, my wife, my sister-in-law Darlynn—who is the wife of Willie, and my sister Delores all worked in the store. Delores was the person responsible for adding wigs to our line of goods which we sold in the store. She felt that it was an item that we could move well. I let her handle that item

My Life and Experiences in the Entertainment World

and it did prove to be of value to the total line of goods that were sold. Some of the female customers would come into the barber shop, have their hair lined up, and after finishing that, they would go next door to our store and purchase a wig. Some would purchase a wig first, then come into the shop to have it cut. So each complimented the other. Of course, there were others who worked in the store at one time or another, but it was the family members who kept everything moving in the right direction.

Being a barber allowed me the opportunity to see and talk with many people from all walks of life. I found that being a shop owner keeps you close to the public and keeps you up to date with all the happenings of the world. I continued writing, too. In the shop you really get an inside track on people. Many patrons really open up to you and expect you to have a solution for all their problems. Some of their problems were very personal, but whatever the problem, they brought it to me. I've always tried to give good and prudent advice to the best of my ability. So the more knowledgeable you are, the easier it is to keep your customers happy.

I found that some customers had problems with drugs, others had problems with alcohol, and many had family problems, even husband and wife problems (or should I say husband and wife disagreements). I would talk and act as an advisor or counselor for them each time they would request that I do so. I was happy to find that I was successful in helping many of them.

I am also proud of the fact that I was able to help some students in the neighborhood with their school work. Many times I acted as a tutor for some of the students. I tried to explain to many the things that confronted them at that time.

Going back to 1963, I had been looking for a new church home. I had been visiting different churches for a while. One day I was in conversation with someone about my seeking a new church home, not only for myself, but for my wife and my child that I wished to bring up properly in a church. So this person invited me to his church. When I visited, I liked it well enough to move my membership there. The name of the church was Bethel Baptist Church East. I enrolled my son Darryl in the church's Sunday School. The pastor had just taken over his duties at the church a short time earlier. His name was Reverend Dr. Carl D. Hughes. I liked him and I saw a lot of good things in him. He was a good leader and teacher. Darryl was baptized by him. The church is located at 5715–21 Holcomb Street on the east side, not far from where I was living at the time. My wife and I are still attending the same church today. Not long after coming there, I joined the Courtesy Committee. Later I became a member of the Sunday School Teaching Staff where I have taught for over thirty years.

Around the same time, I started my music publishing company, so that I could basically publish my songs and have a bigger take of the royalties which came from my songs.

Mertis John

During the time when Nat Cole was ill with cancer in 1963 or 1964, I wrote a song which I had intended to present to him to record. It's titled, "That's You." The song was written in his style. I know he would have liked it because, without a doubt, it fitted him perfectly. I, unfortunately, never had an opportunity to present it to him. After he became ill, he never recovered. He passed away in February of 1965.

Later that summer, Willie's band asked me to write a song for them. The song I wrote was, "Steppin' Out." It was cut in New York City and released by the Fire Record Company. Bobby Robinson headed that company. The name of the band was the Upsetters.

After that, it was time for me to give Willie the next song I had written for him; "So Lovely," a nice easy ballad. That song was followed by, "I Like to See My Baby," which is an up-tempo song. Later, I wrote, "It Only Hurts a Little While" for him.

The songs, "You Hurt Me" and "I Like to See My Baby," were recorded about the same time. Now when I first wrote "I Like to See My Baby," it was not an up tempo composition. However, when we went to the studio to record the session, another of King's artists was there. It happened to be Hank Ballard of "The Twist" fame.

When I presented the song at the session and ran it down for Willie, he said to me, "I think Hank and I should do this song together. He's here. I think we could have some fun doing this one together." He then asked Hank how he would like singing with him. Hank wanted to hear the song. I ran it down for him.

He said, "Yeah, let's do it." Both singers got together then to see how it would come together with two parts. It was decided that the tempo would be changed to an up tempo beat. So we proceeded to record the song, "I Like To See My Baby" in an up tempo beat as it is heard on the released recording. They did have fun doing it.

When I wrote "You Hurt Me," I was trying to write a song that equaled the success of "Fever." Willie really loved the song from the first time that I sang it for him. Everyone in the studio at that time liked it and felt that it would become something big.

Willie stated to me, "Mert, you really wrote the right thing when you wrote that one." I was happy and excited about it, too. The same can be said for the tunes, "Take My Love (I Want To Give It All To You)" and "So Lovely" which I wrote for him and were recorded around the same time in 1961 and 1962.

Mr. Glenn
On February 20, 1962, an American Astronaut named John Glenn became the first American to orbit the earth. He made three orbits which took four hours fifty-five minutes and twenty-three seconds to complete. His spaceship was named *Friendship Seven*, a mercury space capsule. That accomplishment thrust the United States into the space age full force.

THAT'S YOU
MERTIS JOHN
Bb Eb F7
LIPS SO A DOR A BLE EYES SHINE LIKE STARS A
Bb Bb7 Eb G° Bb G-
BOVE HANDS LIKE THE COT TON IN MY PIL LOW
C F Bb
THAT'S YOU THAT'S YOU YOUR VOICE IS LIKE A SONG
Eb Bb Eb G°
SING ING MEL O DIES TO ME SO I TELL MY
Bb Ab G C7 F7 Bb A7 D-
SELF THAT'S YOU THAT'S YOU HOURS AF TER WE'VE
A7 D-
PAR TED THO I'M MA NY MILES A WAY I CAN
G-
STILL FEEL YOUR LIPS TO MINE LIKE IT WAS YES TER
C7 F7 Bb
DAY WHEN WE WALK DOWN THE ISLE
Eb F7 Bb Eb
WEAR ING THAT HEAVEN LY SMILE THAT'S WHEN I'LL TELL MY SELF
Bb Ab G C7 F7 B
THAT'S YOU THAT'S YOU
MERTIS MUSIC CO
BMI
10 Stave
Passantino
Manuscript No. 52
© ℗ 1957 AND 1985

Mertis John

Wanting to keep in step with the time, King Records called Willie into the studio to record a song to commemorate the great step in space that this country had made. When he got to the studio, they had a song called, "Mr. Glenn," for him to record. The storyline tells about John Glenn's historic space exploration and the things he saw and felt in flight as he orbited the earth. The song also expresses the singer's desire to make the flight with him in the future some day.

That recording, I feel, should have sold millions. It should have touched the world to the point that they couldn't get to the record stores fast enough to buy it. But that didn't happen. For what this event meant to the United States and to the rest of the free world, I was very disappointed when the record commemorating it did not burst the charts wide open.

In 1998, Mr. Glenn at age seventy-seven, and the oldest person to go into space, was called on once more. On October 29, 1998, he became a member on board the *Discovery*. The *Discovery* space mission lasted nine days. On this shuttle, John Glenn was the payload specialist and he was given several scientific tests to conduct, one of which was to test the sleeping abilities of older persons in space as opposed to their sleeping abilities on earth.

Before this mission, Mr. Glenn had been out of the NASA Program for a long time. Having resigned in 1964, he went into politics in his hometown of New Concord, Ohio. He was elected to the U.S. Senate in 1974. He made an unsuccessful bid for president in 1984. He was scheduled to retire from the Senate in January of 1999.

In 1996, things seemed to still be going well with all of the family. Mable was now with Stax Records. This was the year that she recorded her first hit, a million seller with that company. She had spent five years with Motown Records before moving on to Stax. Her first big score with Stax was, "Your Good Thing Is About to End." We were all excited about that. My business was doing well too. She and I were talking about the new record, about how it was doing, and how the musicians at Stax bring the musical arrangements together at a record session. "You must go and see," she told me. She wanted me to go with her to her next session. I told her that I would. The next session was scheduled for sometime in June of that year. Before we left, she told my brother Raymond that she wanted him to come along, too. So the three of us left together for the session.

The sessions were run by Isaac Hayes, Booker T. Jones, and David Porter. Isaac and Booker T. did the producing. I met them and the other fine musicians who made up the cooking sounds of Stax Records. Jim Stewart, along with Ms. Estelle Axton, headed up the company as owners. They did go about recording a session differently than I had ever seen. No musical charts or arrangements were written. Instead Isaac, who played the piano, would get the key that was right for the singer, give it to the other musicians, then he would tell the other musicians how it was going to be done. They would fall in, then they would run it down with the singer or

My Life and Experiences in the Entertainment World

singers until it was good enough to test a take. The engineer would get a balance, and they would start rolling from there until they had the final take. They all worked good together and their method was very successful for them.

Another person I met at Stax was Deanie Parker who worked in the office, but she also wrote songs. Some of the artists were Otis Redding, Eddie Floyd, Willie Bell, the Bar-Kays, Johnny Taylor, Rufus Thomas, Albert King, The Staple Singers, Isaac Hayes, Eddie Floyd, William Bell, Carla Thomas, Booker T & The MG's, The Emotions, The Soul Children, and Sam and Dave.

Other musicians who played on the sessions were Steve Cropper, Guitar; Duck Dunn, Bass; Al Jackson, Drums; Booker T., Organ, Trombone, and Horn; and I believe Gilbert Caple or Gene Parker, was on saxophone. Al Bell was doing promotion for the company, and he went on to become the owner and president sometime later.

Musically and businesswise, everything was continuing to go well for the family as a whole, but into the month of November when we all had begun to think and plan for the coming Holiday season, the family was jolted. My mother, all of my sisters and brothers, and I were about to experience something that we had never felt before. It was November 3, 1966, my oldest sister Mable's birthday. I got up and prepared myself to go off to work just as I had done every other workday. I was feeling fine. I continued to feel great all day until I came home and walked in the door. My wife had gotten a call from Mother Dear letting her know that Daddy had passed away. She met me at the door and tried to prepare me for what she had to say. She started by saying, "I have some news to tell you. I want you to be strong because the news isn't good." I told her to go ahead and tell me. Then she told me that Daddy had passed away. Suddenly everything changed. I felt as if the world had ended. No one in the John household had died until now.

The first thing I did was to get on the phone and call Mother Dear. She confirmed that he had passed away. Then she said, "Mert, I want you to take care of everything." I assured her that I would. The next thing that I did was to call Mable. She was not in the city. We began to discuss how we would do what was to be done. Along with my wife and son, I drove over to my mother's home to be with the rest of the family. Mable came in the following day. It was very hard to believe that our dad, the family leader, would not be with us anymore. During those days of sorrow, we certainly received a lot of support from Berry Gordy. He was at my mother's house every day, which helped a great deal. He went all the way for us. I'll always remember and be grateful to him for being there for us. Also, I want to mention here too, that the family also received a great deal of support from a very popular radio disk jockey at the time, Martha Jean—The Queen. She visited my home and she was with us all the way. To her, I'll always be grateful as well.

Mertis John

The next day we went to meet with the funeral director to make all the plans for dad's burial. I held up very well until the very last minute, at the grave site. As the casket was being lowered I became weak. I found myself reaching down to try and pull the casket back up. Then I realized I couldn't. Then the feeling began to go away. I suddenly began to feel that I would never see Daddy again. Through the entire ordeal I experienced my weakest moment then and there at the end.

We finally got back home, and the day ended. The following day I began to resume my normal schedule. I felt better if I kept busy. The holiday season was a few days away. We went ahead doing as we had always done, getting through the season. But it sure felt different not having Daddy around, and knowing that he would not be in our presence again.

Soon we were into a new year, 1967, and I had decisions confronting me. I had attended college earlier but I had not finished. My mind was restless, so I had to stay busy. I wanted to return to school, but I needed to find the time to fit it into my already busy schedule. If I should return, how would I find time to write songs? Well, I decided to return to school. I would major in business and English. During those two years, I had to divorce myself from writing. It was a hard decision to make, but that was the right decision to make. I certainly could not keep up with all the things that I was doing. I didn't write songs for those two years.

I continued to work during the day, and at night I would attend classes. When I'm doing things that I like, I am very eager. It was no different with my going to school. I carried a full load of classes since I wasn't writing songs. However, I did take a creative writing course that would allow my creative juices to flow and remain active. Consequently, I was able to write a lot of poetry and short stories. I enjoyed it enormously! Studying that course enabled me to eventually write poetry for various publications and later have my own book of poetry published. As I look back on it, I'm pleased to have made that decision. Later in life, I had the opportunity to speak before large groups of poets and attendees for three years at poetry conventions. The years were 1989, 1990, and 1991.

My first love is writing songs; it has been since I was a teenager. I suppose my second is writing poetry. But keep in mind, one has to be a good poet in order to be a good songwriter, so I would say my first and second loves go hand-in-hand.

After I was finished with my schooling, I returned to my first love, writing songs. I also applied at the Detroit Board of Education for employment and was hired. While teaching, I continued writing songs, but my employment with the Detroit Public Schools System lasted for thirty years, at which time I retired.

In 1976, my sister Mable had a plan to produce a television talk show. She wanted to be the show's host. She named the show, "Inside Music." She would have a list of top entertainers and others in the business such as actors, musicians, record company executives, writers, and show and

E. M. TURNER SCHOOL

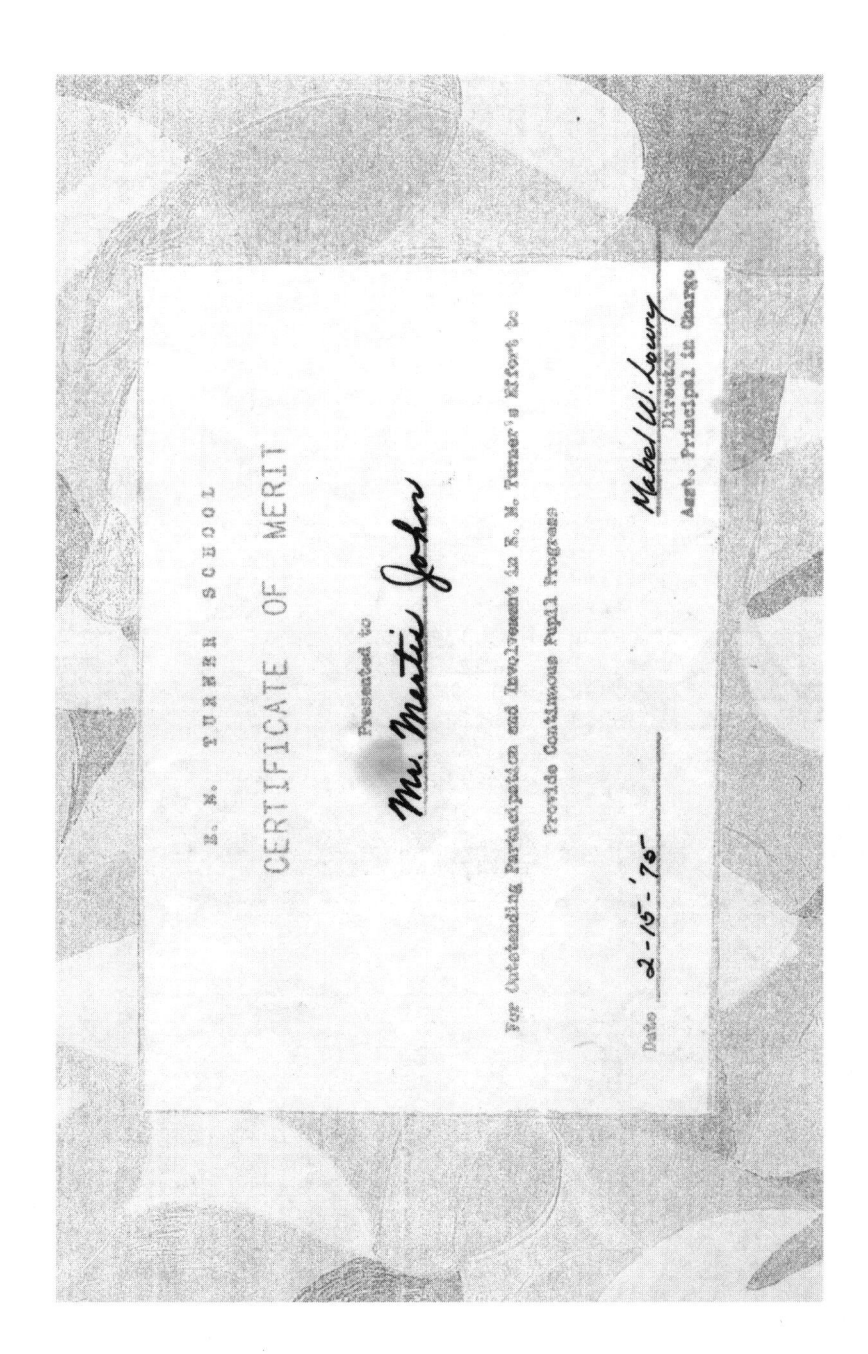

CERTIFICATE OF MERIT

Presented to

Mrs. Martin John

For Outstanding Participation and Involvement in E. M. Turner's Effort to
Provide Continuous Pupil Progress

Date 2-15-'75

Mabel W. Lowry
Director
Asst. Principal in Charge

DETROIT PUBLIC SCHOOLS
REGION FIVE
TURNER ELEMENTARY SCHOOL
14900 PARKSIDE   DETROIT, MICHIGAN 48238   PHONE 864-0017

June 10, 1975

Mr. Mertis John
Turner School
14900 Parkside
Detroit, Michigan

Dear Mr. John:

The Career Awareness Committee is very grateful for your fine presentation on songwriting. The assembly enjoyed your music, the sharing of your personal experiences as well as memories of your brother, Little Willie John.

Thank you.

Sincerely,

Ann Merritt
Ann Merritt, Chairman
Turner School Career Awareness Committee

Mabel W. Lowry
Mabel W. Lowry
Administrator

MWL:ma

My Life and Experiences in the Entertainment World

movie producers as guests who would come on the show and discuss the many things that go on backstage behind the scenes. She had a good concept for the show, so she called me from Hollywood to explain every aspect about it to me. Then she asked me if I wanted to be a part of the production. Of course I told her that I would, so I flew out to Hollywood to be at the taping and also to perform my obligations. That was an exciting and fun-filled experience.

We had hoped to syndicate the show so that it would be seen nationally, but because of a lack of sponsorship, the show never got that far. I suppose we were ahead of our time with that project. I returned home, but a short time after, something happened to our marriage. The harmony that I had known was no longer present. We began to argue and disagree on almost everything. For some unexplained reason, I could no longer please the woman I had married almost twenty years before. Not even after buying a new car for her. The following year, our marriage was over. I didn't want it to end. I had felt early on that it never would. Our son, Darryl, would graduate from Cass Technical High School the following year and go on to college. However, the reality was that our marriage had fallen apart. I subsequently moved out of the home and continued my life on a positive note. I eventually was married a second time to Olivia Fuller. However, that marriage ended in a divorce as well. Now my current marriage has been nothing short of a marriage made in heaven. We both enjoy true wedding bliss; our honeymoon has never ended. We both feel that God has joined us together and that we will always be. "If at first you don't succeed, try, try again." My current wife and the love of my life is Verlaine.

That's the way my life has gone. I kind of look back on my life as similar to Job. I think of how he was a rich man and then lost everything that he had. In his losses and in what happened to be his misfortune, he never looked back. He waited on God and he always persevered and looked to God, for he knew all blessings come from God. So God blessed him above and beyond what he had possessed before because he continued to trust Him. So what most people would describe as misfortune turned out to be good fortune for Job, a tremendous blessing.

So it is with me. I have given up a lot as I sojourned in life, but I kept smiling. I waited and persevered; I didn't look back on what was gone. I kept reaching up and moving forward knowing if I continued to do the right thing, God's blessings would follow me. Now I am blessed beyond any measure that I had been in the past. God has really smiled on me. Whatever it may be that you lose in life, or fail to reach, don't feel that all is lost and that it's over for you. It certainly does not have to be so.

While working in the Carolinas in 1964, the police visited Willie's dressing room. While there they found a small amount of marijuana in the room. He was arrested and charged. Later, he had to appear before a judge. The judge admonished him and his judgment was that he pay a fine and further told him to stay out of any further trouble with respect to the

Mertis John

law. Then he went on to say, "If you should get into trouble with the law in the future, you will do some time." After the fine was paid, Willie was released.

The next day he resumed his schedule of dates. He played the remaining dates on this tour and worked through the territories of the country that would take him to the West Coast. He then worked up the west coast of California after dates in Denver, Nevada, and Arizona. The next show would be in Seattle, Washington. He played the show then after it was over, like so many other times before, he was invited to an after party. I personally didn't care for those parties and I tried many times to discourage him from going to them. I always told him instead of going to the parties, to go get some rest. But Willie loved to be at parties; that night was no exception. While at the party that night, some kind of scuffle occurred. While this was taking place, a man who was involved in the scuffle was struck with a small knife. He was taken to the hospital but later died. To my knowledge, the knife was never found.

In 1965, Willie was arrested and charged with manslaughter. I tried everything I could to keep him out. I put up $10,000.00 for bond. He was released on bond, and he went back to work. He even came home during that time and played one of the popular clubs, the Phelps Lounge. But his court date awaited him. When his court date came, he flew to Seattle. During the trial, it was never proven that it was he who stuck the deceased, but Willie's past came back to haunt him.

The judge looked back into his past record and the judgment he handed down was this: "You need to be taken off your feet for a while. I'm going to put you away for three years. I'm remanding you to the prison at Walla Walla, Washington, for that specified time." So with that, Willie was on his way to prison.

I was devastated. We stayed in touch while he was there. He always told us not to worry about him and that he would be alright. While there, he wrote some songs that he had planned to record after his release. While he was still there in 1967, he was allowed to travel to Capitol Records in Los Angeles to record an album. He was still under contract with King Records. However, Capitol Records wanted him and was hoping that they cold buy his contract from King Records. But, Sid Nathan at King Records stood firm and said he wouldn't sell Willie's contract to anyone, no matter who. So there they were, having recorded what I felt was Willie's best album but could not release it.

We didn't like the situation but there wasn't anything that anyone could do but wait. Unfortunately, that album turned out to be Willie's last recording. I had started writing new songs for him when it was coming up to the time for his release. His release was scheduled for July 19, 1968. He came very close to enjoying it, but he was not fortunate enough to make it. He was only seven weeks short of being released.

I looked back on the many things that we had done and shared together. They were all clouded now with so much sorrow and a constant hurting inside me. As I look now thinking over the plans we had made for the future, and I am again saddened because we will never be able to do any of those things that we were looking forward to. Most of all, I'm saddened because of the fact that Willie had to leave us here on earth so soon and I, along with the rest of the family, and your lovely family that you had made, your wife Darlynn and your sons, Kevin and Keith, cannot enjoy being with you as we all loved to do so much.

On the other hand, we still have you. We will always have you in our hearts, as well as in our minds. A song will always remain in my heart for you. We have something even now, that other loved ones left behind don't have. We can hear your voice loud and clear by playing your records and feel your presence by watching you on film. Those are things of which to be thankful for.

Chapter Thirteen

The songs that I was writing for Willie he would never sing, see, or hear. The songs he had written and was waiting to record, he can never record. On the morning of May 26, 1968, Little Willie John passed away peacefully in his sleep. Tragedy had entered the John Family once more. I had gone to church that Sunday morning, after which I went to the record store to open it for the day. Soon after I arrived, I received a phone call. I answered it; it was Mother Dear. I was glad to hear her voice. I greeted her as I always did. I thought she wanted to know if I would be over later. Usually each Sunday I went over to visit her. She said, "Mert, I have some sad news for you."

I asked, "What is it Mother Dear?"

Then she said, "Willie passed away this morning in his sleep."

"Are you sure?" I asked her. She said she was sure. We talked on for a short time longer. Feeling more sadness than I could ever explain, I told her I would see her later after I closed the store.

Then later, the news began to spread. People were coming into the store offering condolences to me. The next thing I did was to call my sister-in-law, Darlynn. After we talked for a while, I knew that she wanted me to go on and take care of certain business. I got the name of the person who was the funeral director on the West Coast to speak with so that he could fly his body home. After completing that, his body arrived at the airport the following evening. The funeral director here drove us to the airport so that we would be there when the body arrived. The body was driven to the funeral home here in Detroit as we followed. No plans were made until the following day.

Phone calls started coming in, people inquiring about his death and about the schedule of services for him. Radio stations, newspapers, record

My Life and Experiences in the Entertainment World

companies, entertainers, and various other people who were connected with the business were all contacting us. Two days of public viewing were scheduled at the funeral home during which time, thousands came to view the body. Then the funeral was held the following day at the New Bethel Baptist Church at Linwood and Philadelphia. The church was pastored by the Reverend C. L. Franklin, singer Aretha Franklin's father's church. Reverend Franklin also preached the eulogy.

The church was packed beyond capacity for the funeral and thousands more stood outside the church on the streets. Condolences came in from all over the world. Disc jockeys, programmers, entertainers, recording executives, the media, television, radio, as well as newspapers and other publications, many friends, and well-wishers all expressed condolences.

A short time later, my sister Mable talked to the family about the possibility of staging a memorial program for Willie. We all felt that it was a great idea. So she started to plan it. She contacted people in the business, such as entertainers, disc jockeys, community leaders, etc., and business people who would participate in the program. After all the participants had assured her that they would appear, she lined up the date and place of the program. She secured the Veterans Memorial Building in Downtown Detroit. The date selected was November 3, 1968.

On November 3, 1968, Mable's birthday, we celebrated a memorial to one of the greatest entertainers the world has ever known, "Little Willie John." Some of the artists who performed were:

Joe Tex	Johnny Taylor
Renae Jackson	Sam & Dave
Eddie Floyd	Don Hart
Johnny Mae Matthews	Little Milton
The Combinations	Lee Dorsey

Reverend Clinton Levert, Jr. and Daughters
Reverend and Madame Edwin G. Robinson and Combo

and Others:

Disc Jockeys From Detroit:

Ernie Durham	Larry Dan
Martha Jean, The Queen	Lee Garrett
Joe Howard	Ray Henderson
Sonny Carter	Ken Bell
Bill Williams	Bristoe Bryant
Wash Allen	

Disc Jockeys From Out of Town:
Lucky Cordell, Assistant Manager of WVGN Radio, Chicago

Remembering My Brother

(Little Willie John)

I had a brother who was born to entertain
Little Willie John was his name to fame
Oh, how he could sing and dance
He was always ready to entertain

It all started when he was about four
He would sing for coins, then ask, "Do you want more?"
On center stage he was right at home
All the ladies loved him, and called him their own

He traveled here and traveled there
They wanted him just about everywhere
Entertaining and making people happy
With him, that's all that really mattered

He had a string of hit records that he would sing
Entertaining was his favorite thing
He was truly–born to entertain
Using his God-given talent and reaching for fame

He was small in stature, but stood out in a crowd
He always said he would make mother proud
"You know I can sing, I'll make lots of money
I'll buy you a home with some of the money."

His one ambition was to entertain
To sing songs to those who needed to lose their inner pain
To hold an audience spellbound while he entertained
He did this well–for he was born to entertain.

Copyright 1996
By Mertis John

My Life and Experiences in the Entertainment World

Some of the John's family also joined in on the entertainment. Mable, Raymond, Haywood, Toronto, and I were all onstage singing.

Sometime shortly following the memorial for Willie, Mable was called by the genius himself, Mr. Ray Charles, and she was asked to become the leader and director of his singing group, the Raylettes. She accepted the offer and remained with him for nine years. After leaving Ray, she returned home. She then set up her own music publishing company. While keeping and running the company, she also began to administer twenty-one other publishing companies, including my company, Mertis Music Company.

In 1985, she entered the Crenshaw Christian Center School of Ministry, from which she graduated. In 1994, she received her Doctorate of Divinity. Also on February 26, 1994, she and I traveled to New York City where she was awarded the R&B Pioneer Award by the Rhythm and Blues Music Foundation. We were joined in New York by our foreign sub-publisher from England, Jeffrey Kruger and his wife René.

Currently, Mable is the pastor of Joy In Jesus Ministries in Los Angeles, California. In addition, she runs the Joy Community Outreach program to end homelessness. She feeds many hungry and gives clothing to many in need.

Earlier in the book, I spoke about how Mable loves to talk. Well, being involved in the things that she came to be involved in, talking became an asset for her, as a tool that made her more qualified and prepared for the task which she subsequently took on in the community in the city of Los Angeles.

In 1979 and 1980, I decided to test some of the skills that I had acquired in college in the creative writing classes. I entered some of my poetry which, if accepted, would be included in an anthology. My presentations were accepted and became a part of the publication. This same process was repeated over the next five years. I also received offers from other publications and agents of the book publishing business. I thought it over and decided to have my first book published. That is when I put together the book, *Speaking From The Heart.* It was published in 1996. Before I had written the book, I had received several awards for my writing, and people urged me to continue. This helped me come to the decision that it was time for me to write my first book.

Thank you so much for your thoughtful gift. I am grateful for your generosity. Your support means a great deal to me as I work to move our nation forward.

Bill Clinton

```
          FROM
  President Bill Clinton
  after receiving my book
  "Speaking From The Heart"
          1997
```

MUSEUM of AFRICAN AMERICAN HISTORY

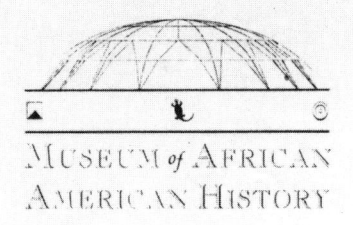

June 6, 1997

Mr. Mertis John
Meda Records Inc.
Detroit, MI 48221

Dear Mr. John,

The Louise Lovett Wright Research Library of the Museum of African American History (MAAH) would like to thank you for your generous donation of "Speaking from the heart". The book will be an invaluable enchancement to our museum collection.

Attached you will find two copies of the Deed of Gift form. Please sign, date and return the **original** copy to the museum, and retain the second copy for your records.

Again, thank you for your support, and for selecting our museum as a repository for your gift.

Sincerely,

Margaret Ward

Margaret Ward
Librarian/Archivist

MY PIANO

This piano has been my number one buddy in my writing career since the early 1950's. I purchased it from The Grinnell Brothers Music store that was then located on Woodward Avenue, in the heart of Downtown Detroit.

I practiced on it, and I also wrote most of my songs on it as well. When my son, Darryl begun studying the piano, this is the one he also used to practice on.

I feel that I owe a great deal to my buddy----
My piano.

        Please write the above under the
        picture of the piano.

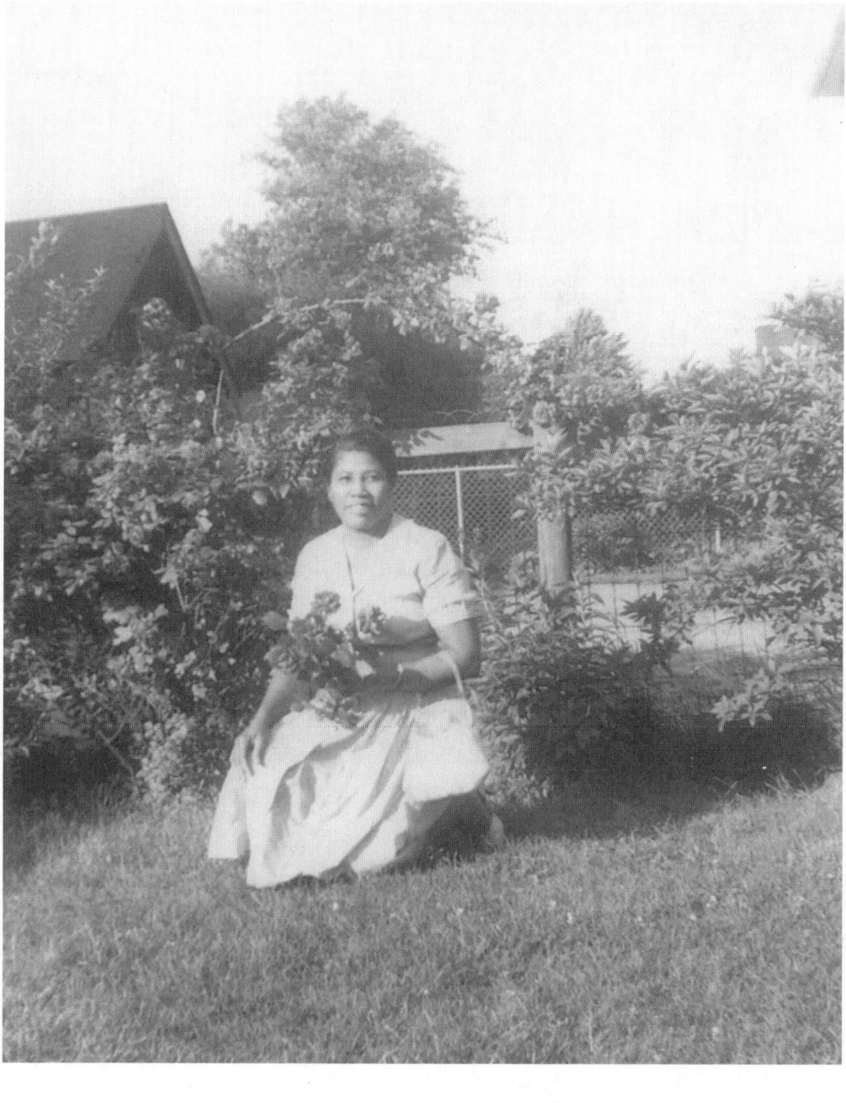

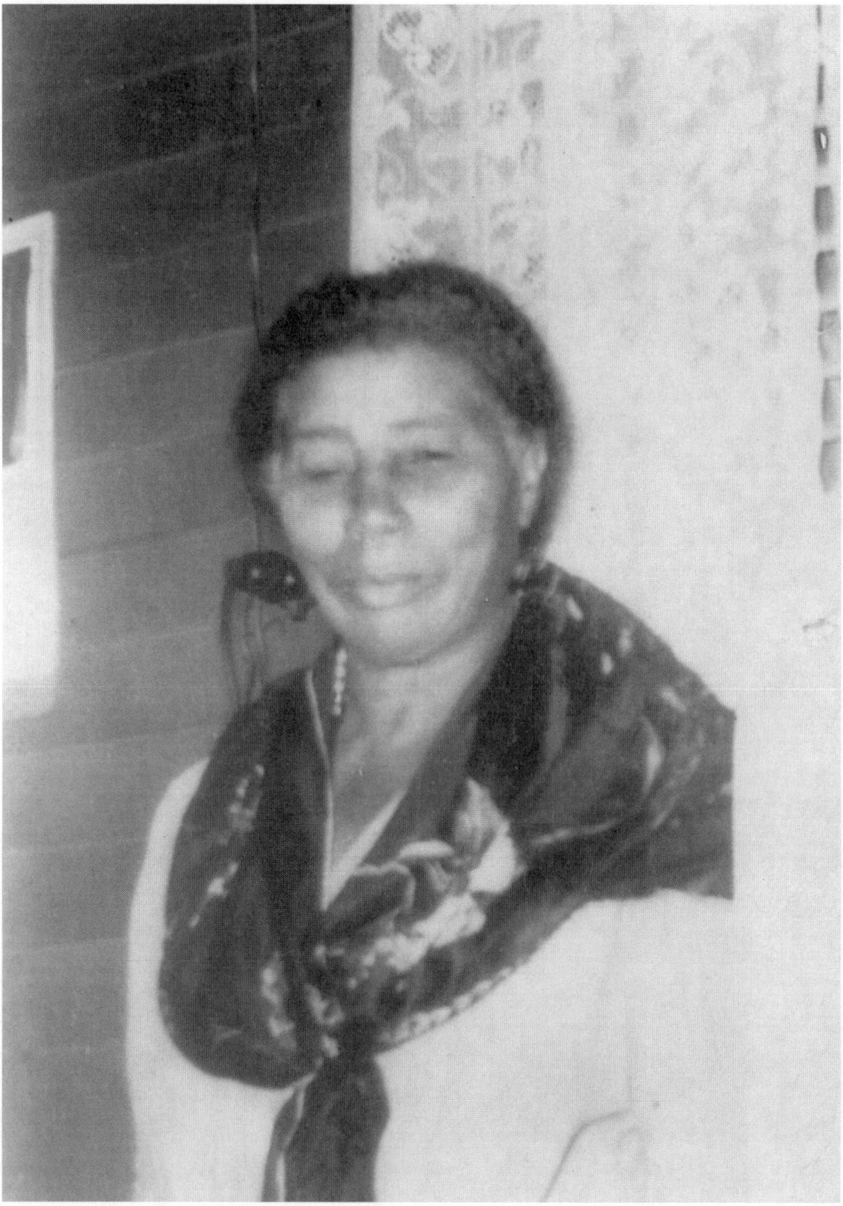

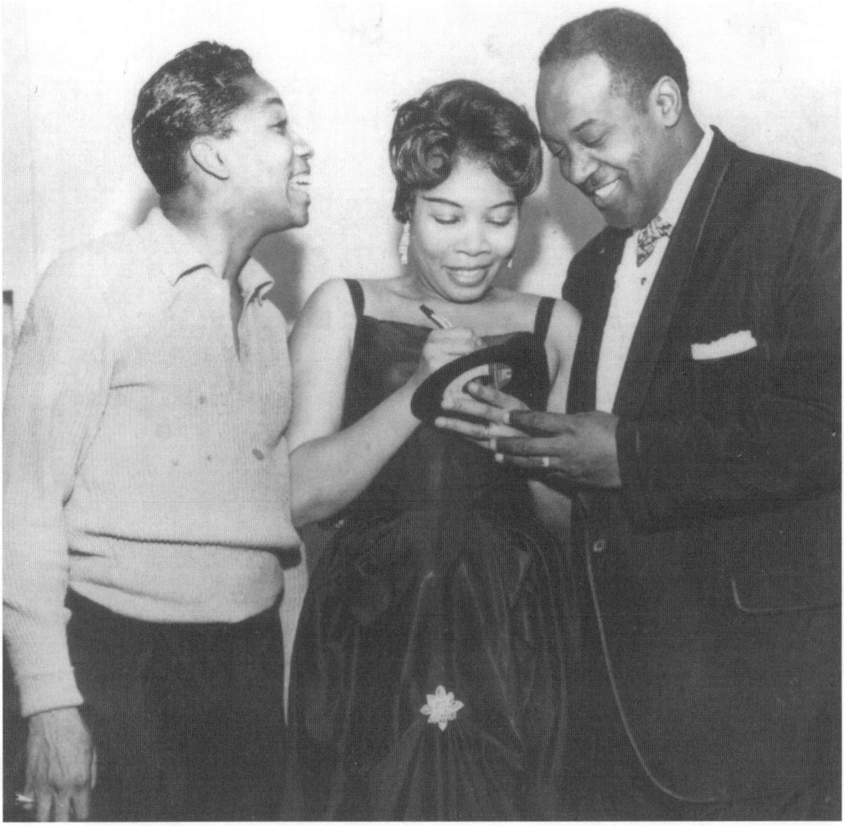

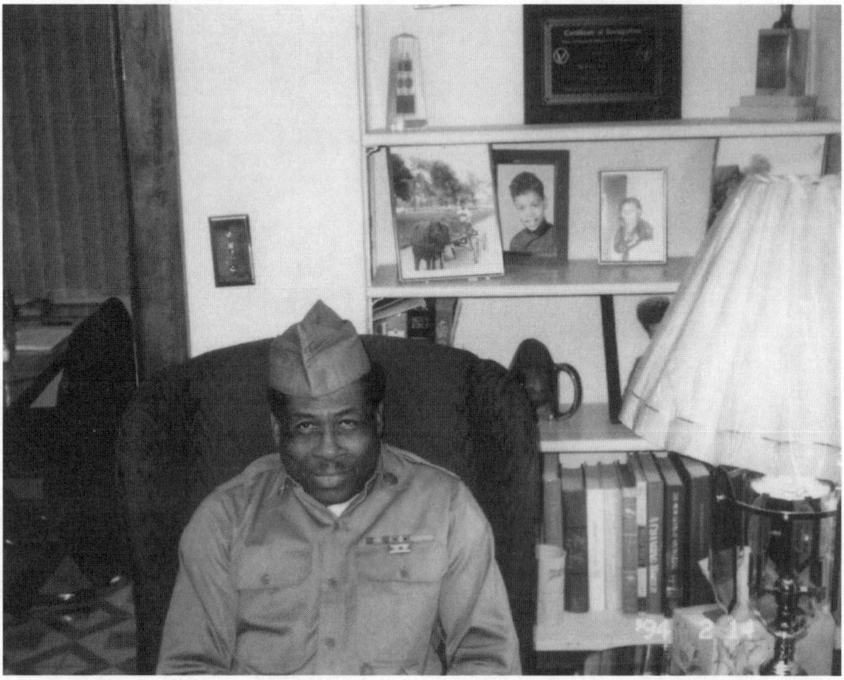

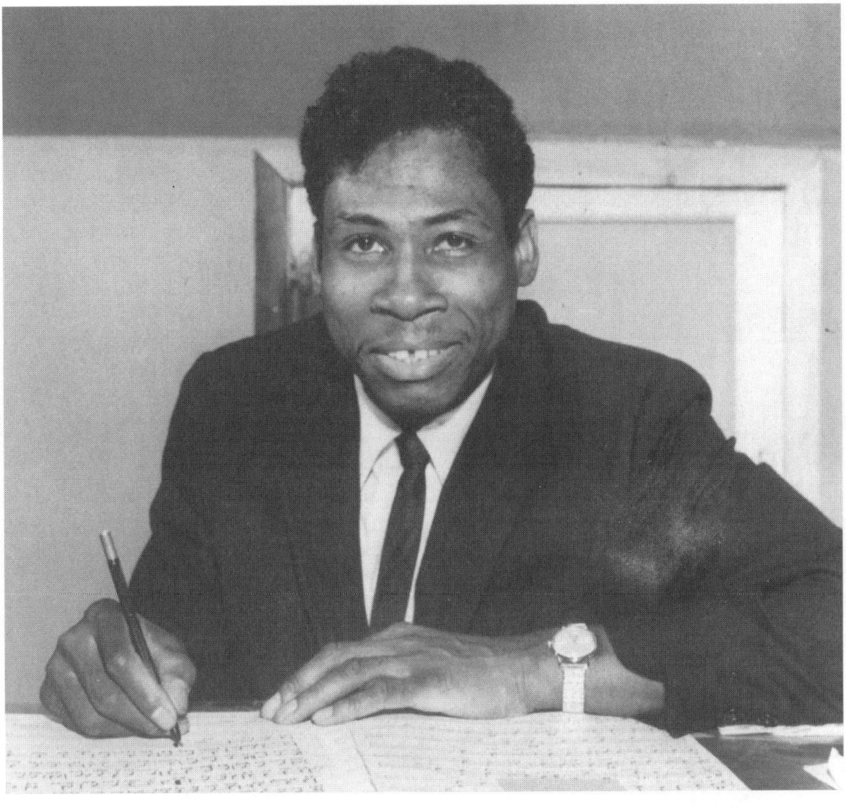

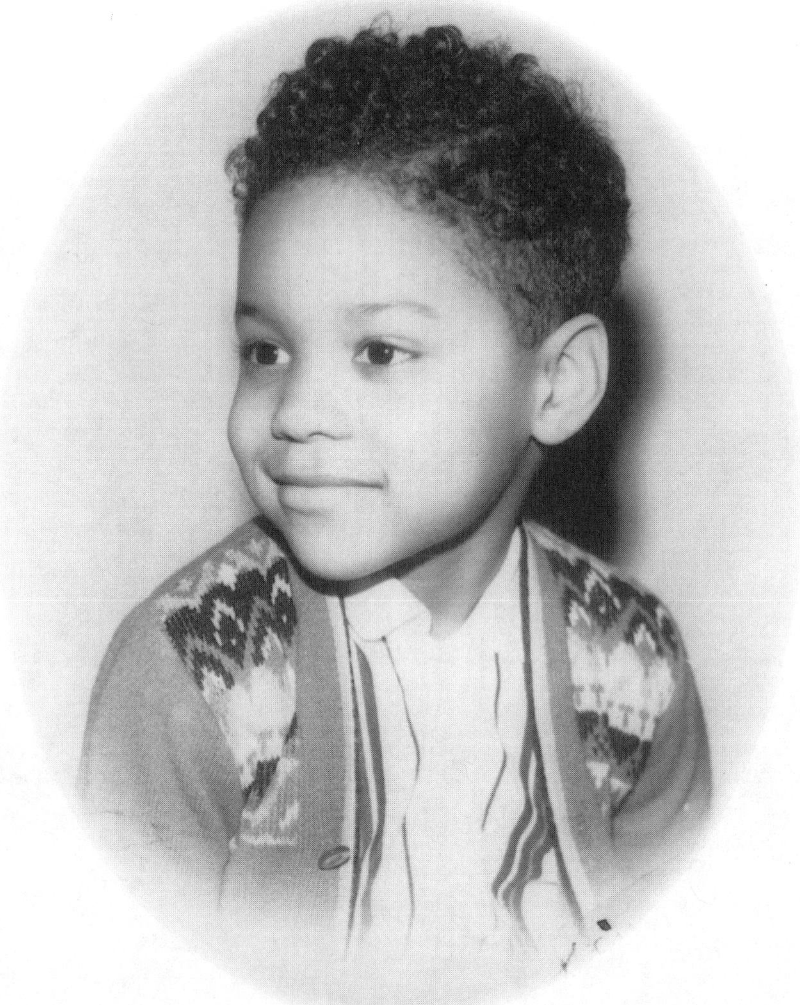

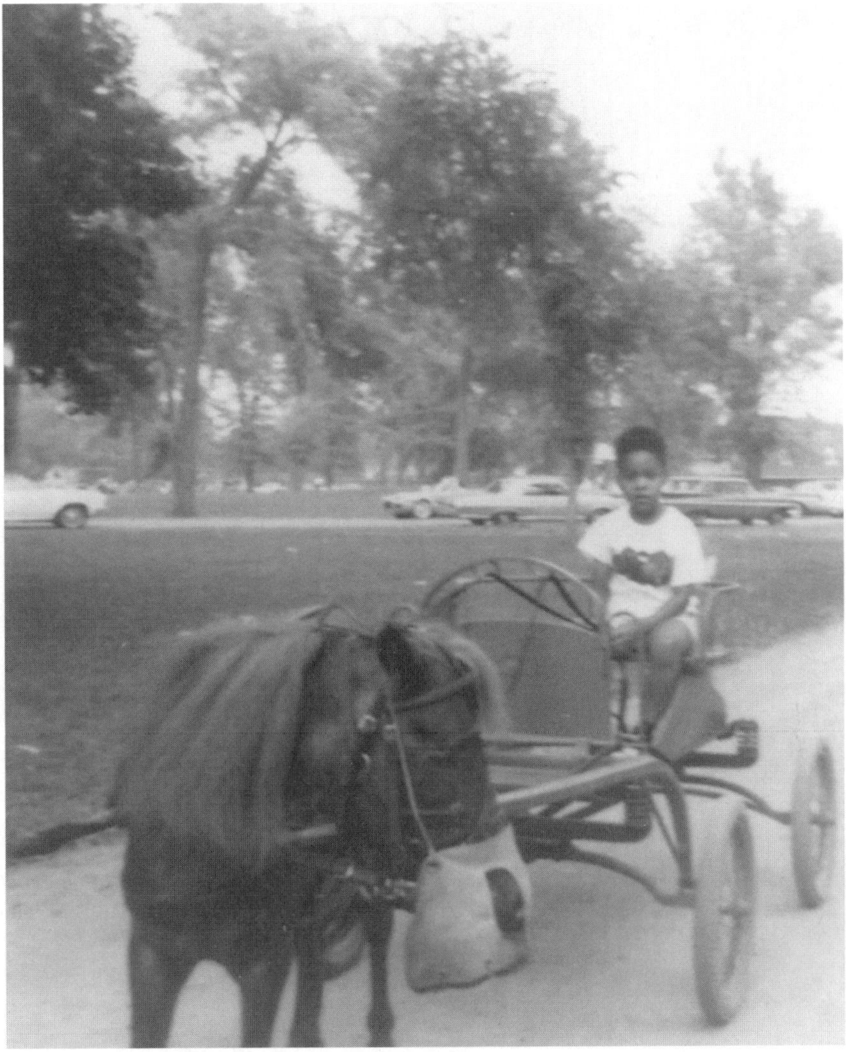

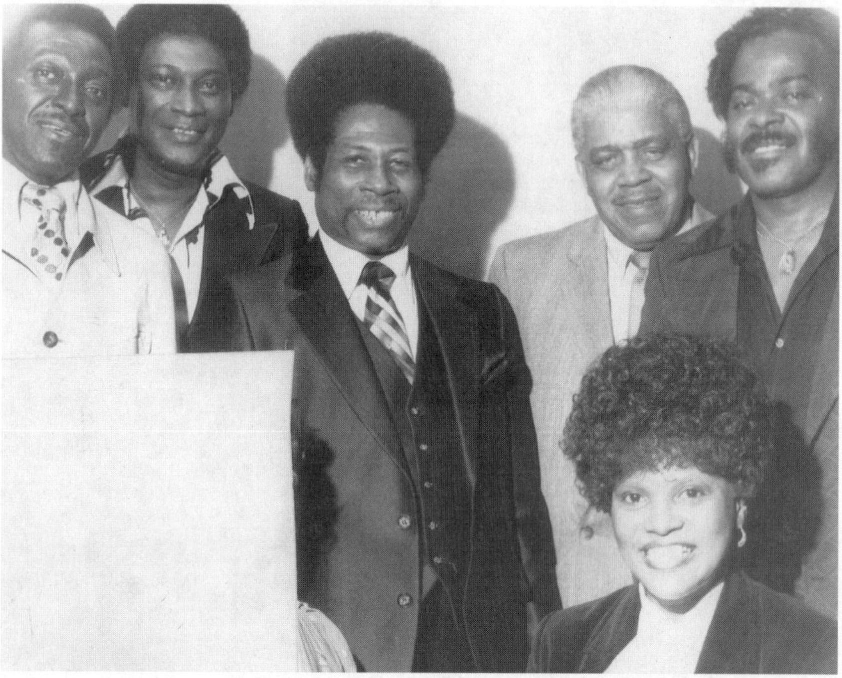

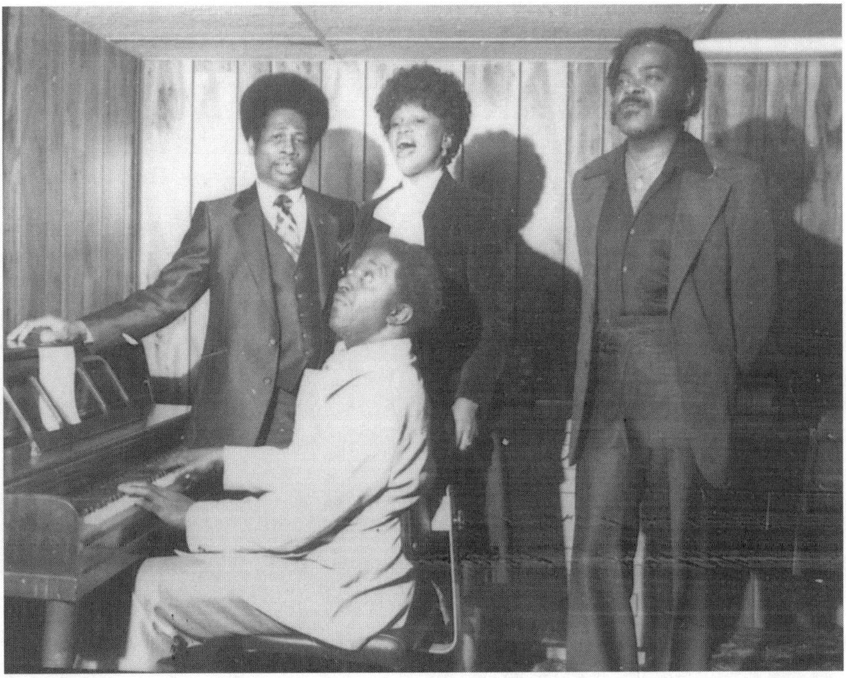

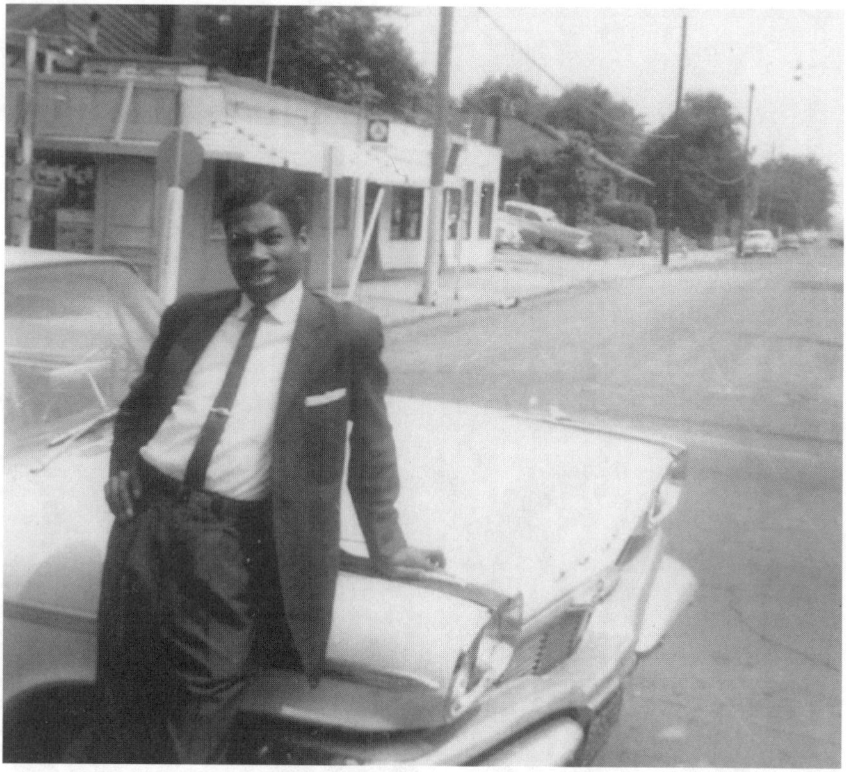

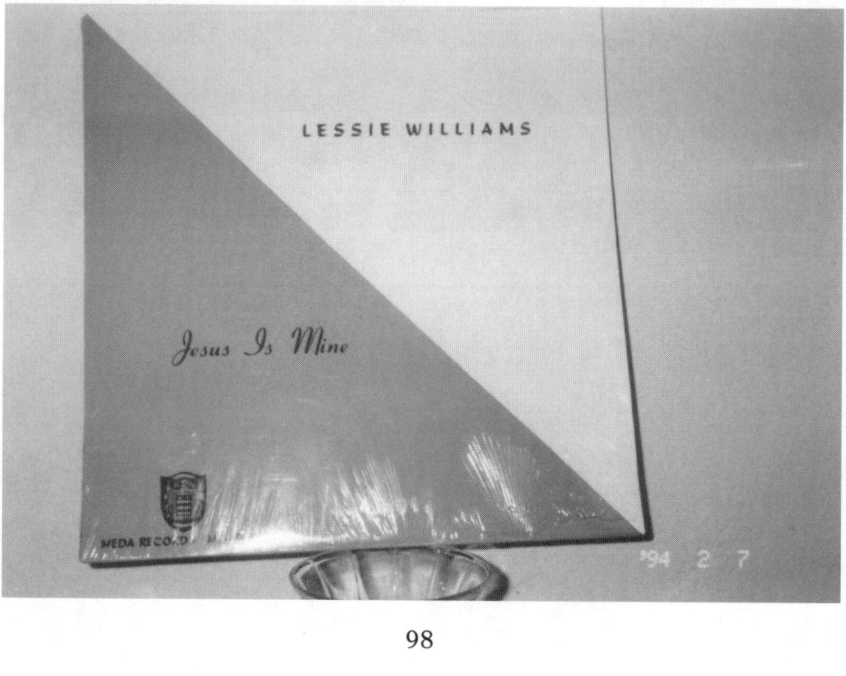
LESSIE WILLIAMS
Jesus Is Mine
'94 2 7

99

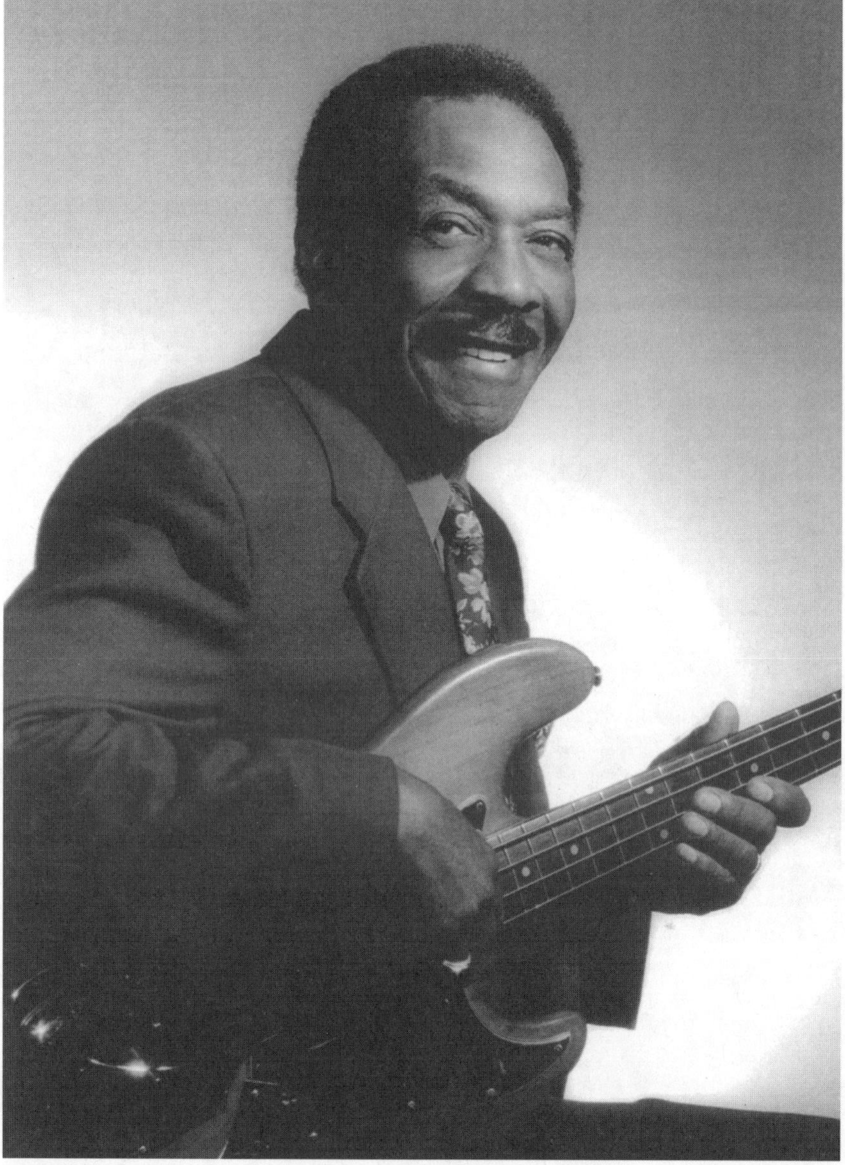

101

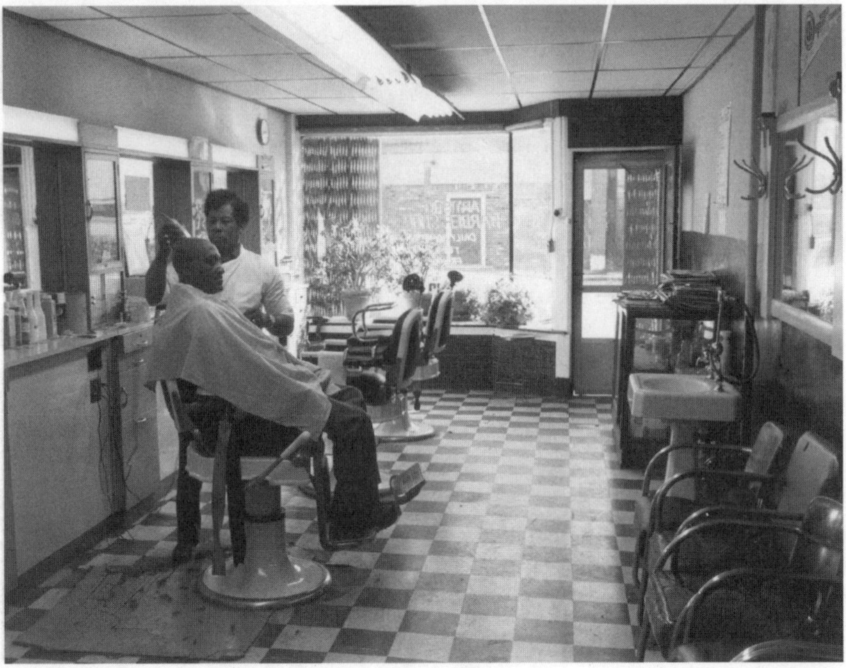

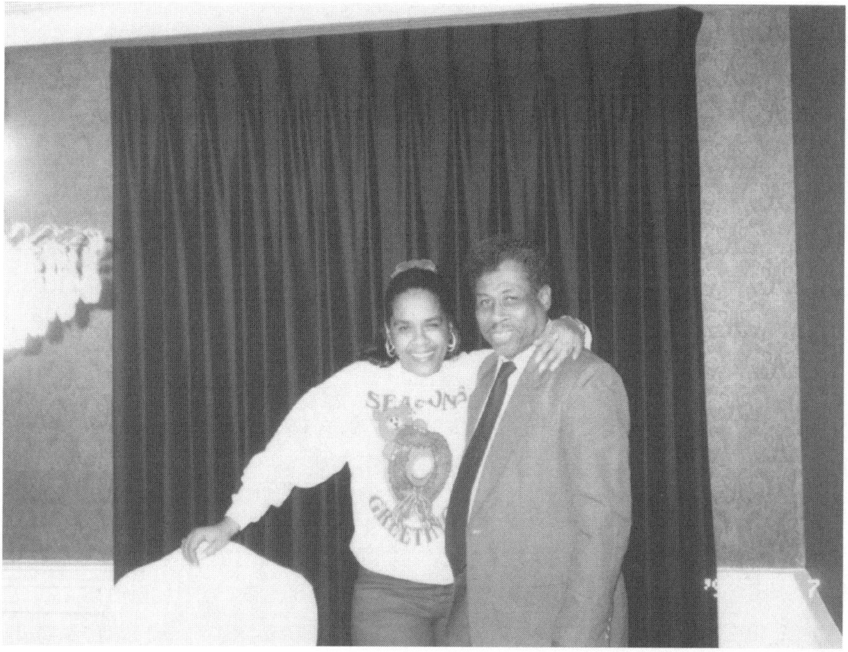

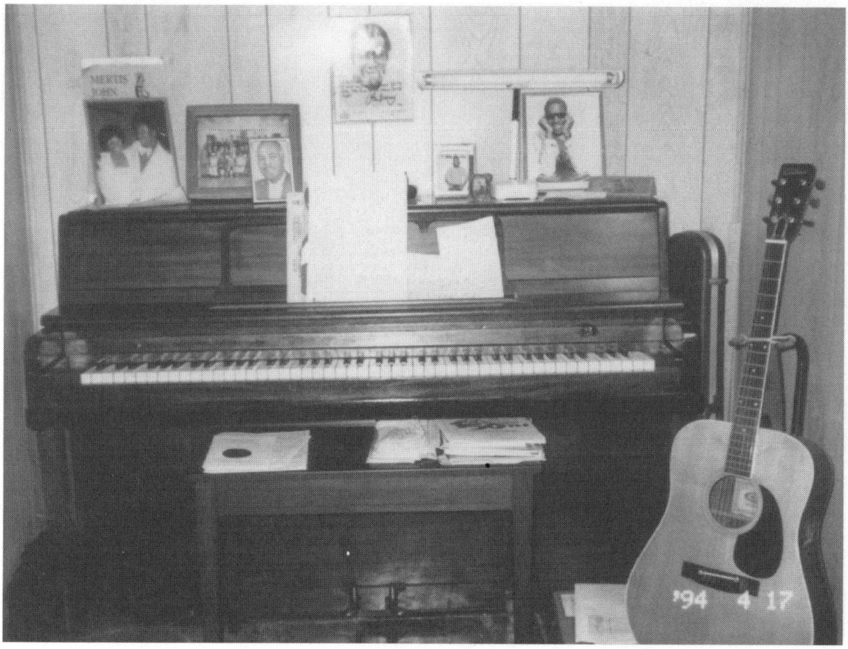
MERTIS
JOHN
'94 4 17

Certificate of Recognition
The United States of America
Mertis John
"Speaking From The Heart"

This is to certify that
Mertis John
was elected into
The International Poetry Hall of Fame
In honor of this election, the
Mertis John Poetry Exhibit
has been established in The International Poetry Hall of Fame Museum.
This exhibit is located at
on the Internet's World Wide Web.
Alex Harley

MICHIGAN
STATE
XXL
HOCKEY

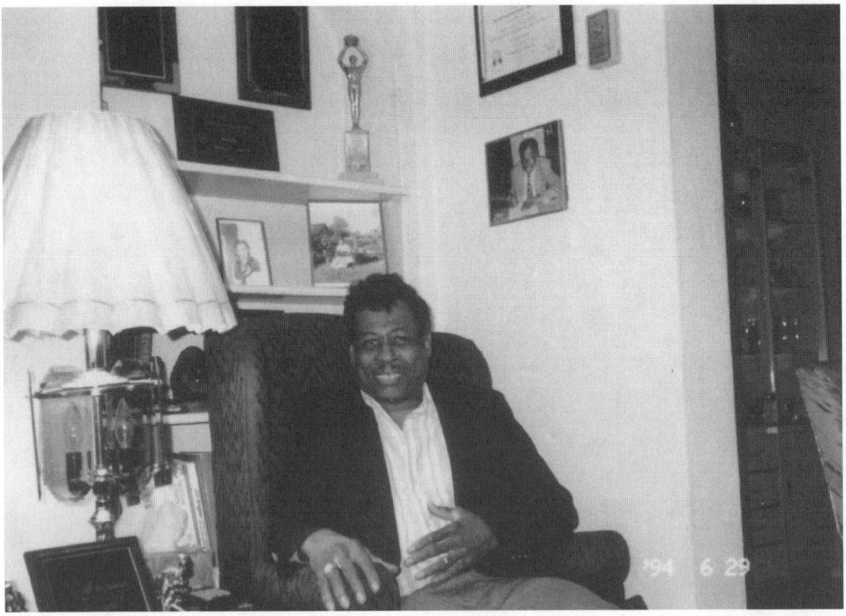
'94 6 29

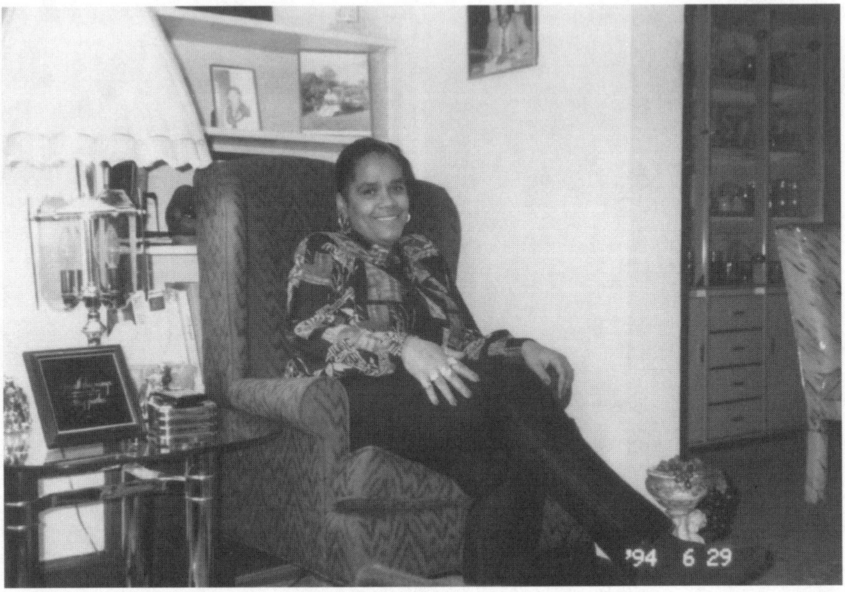
'94 6 29

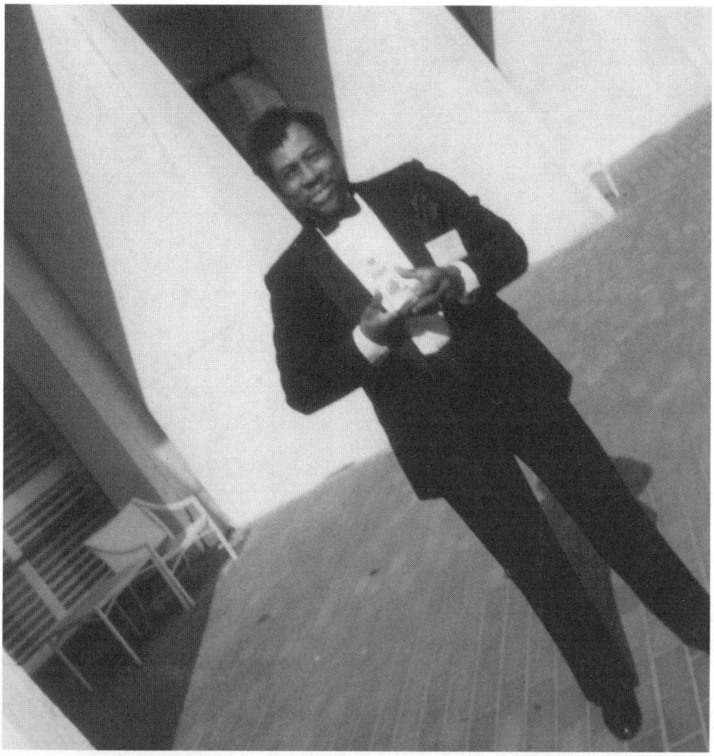

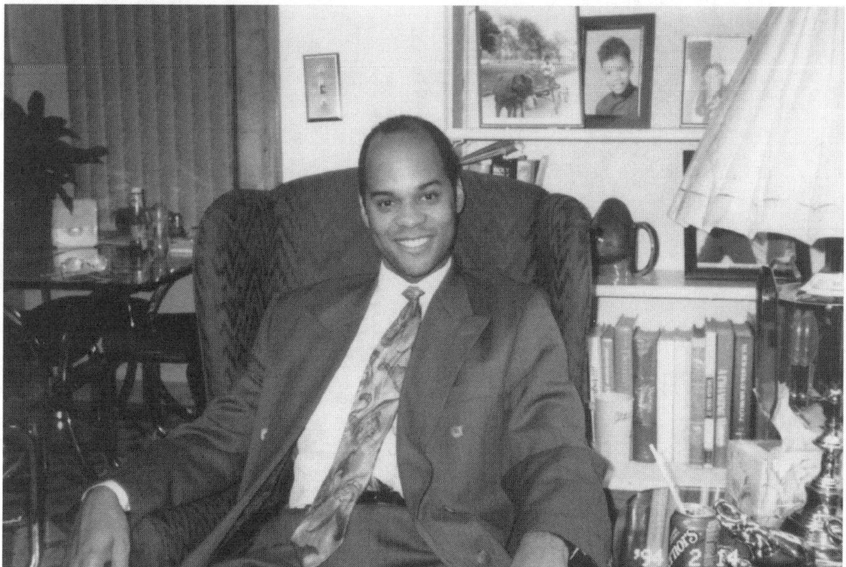
'94 2 14

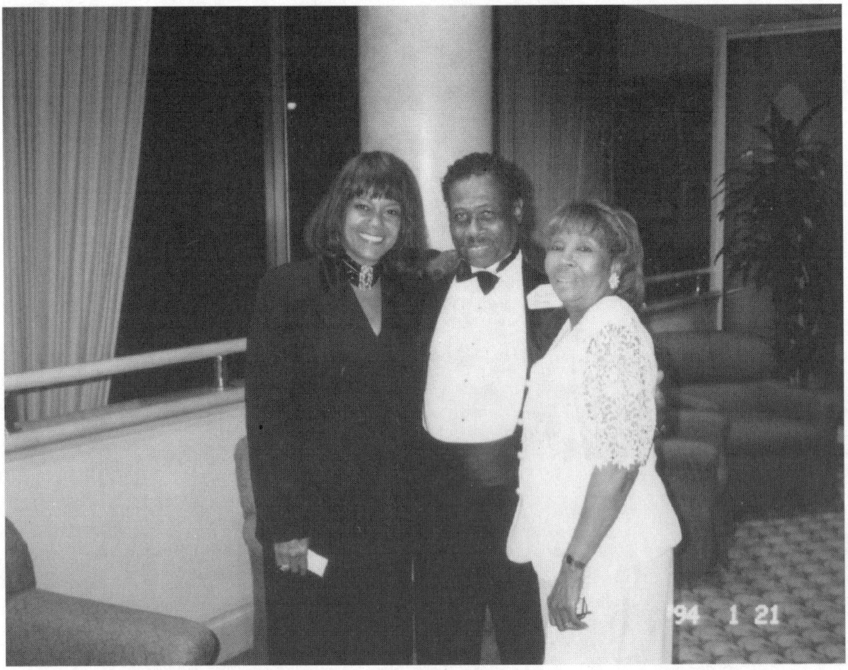
'94 1 21

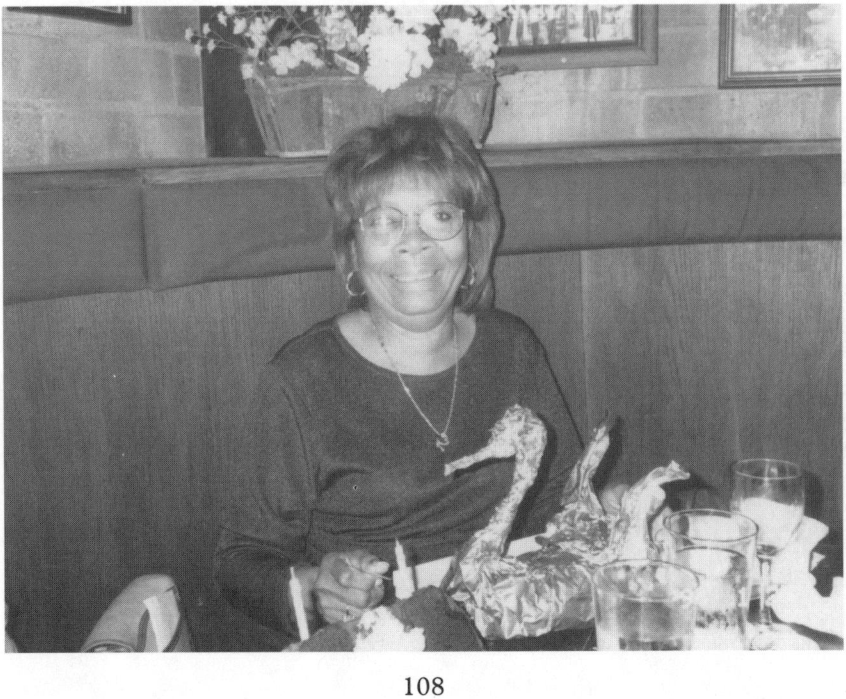

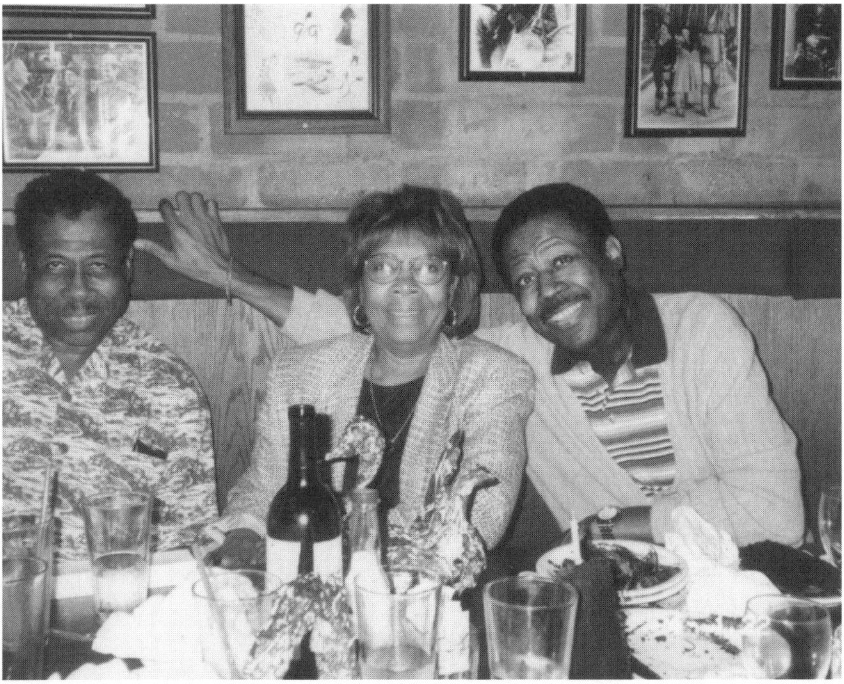

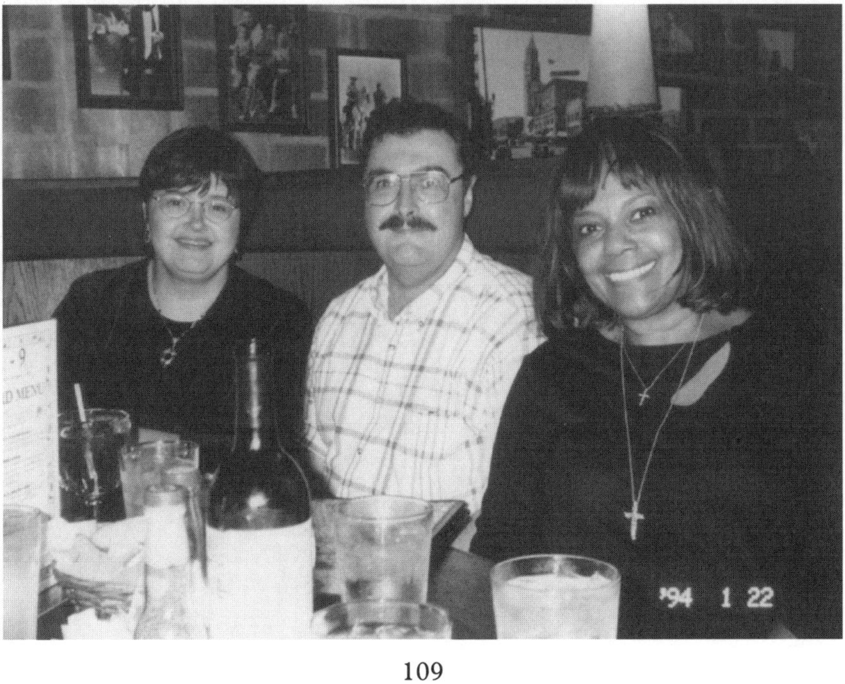
'94 1 22

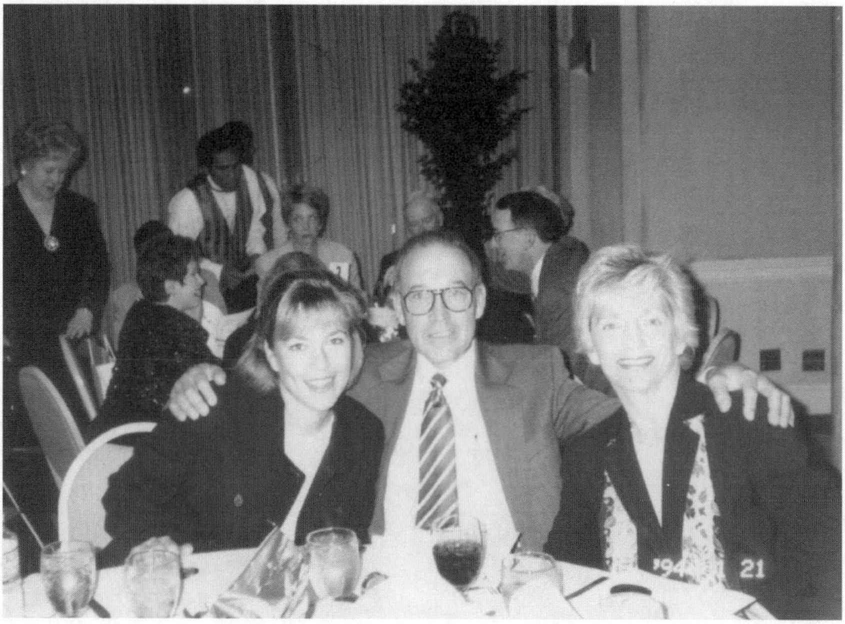

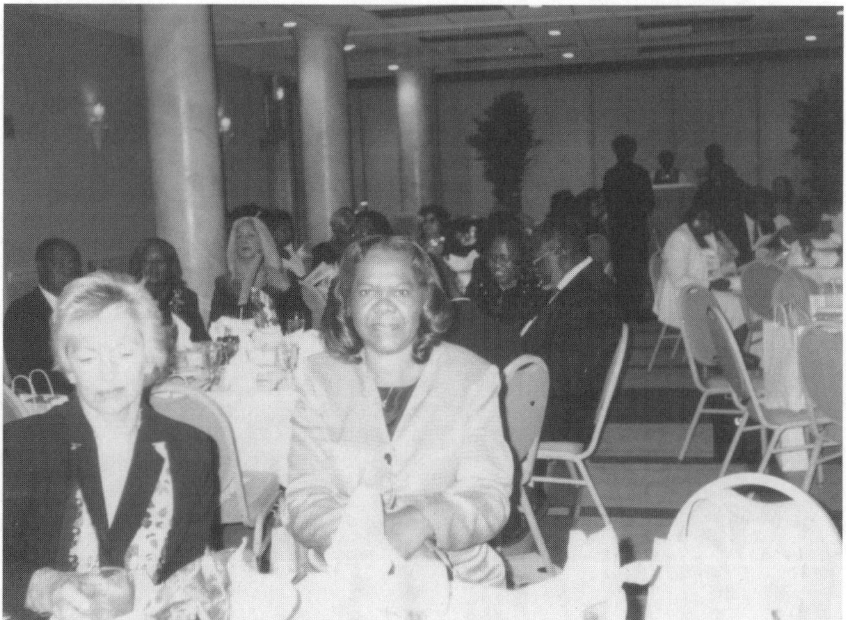

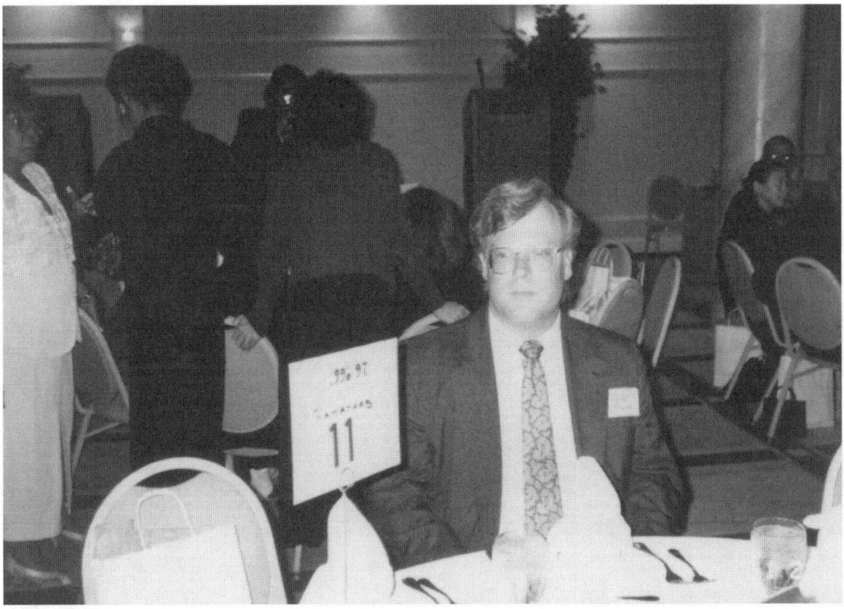
11

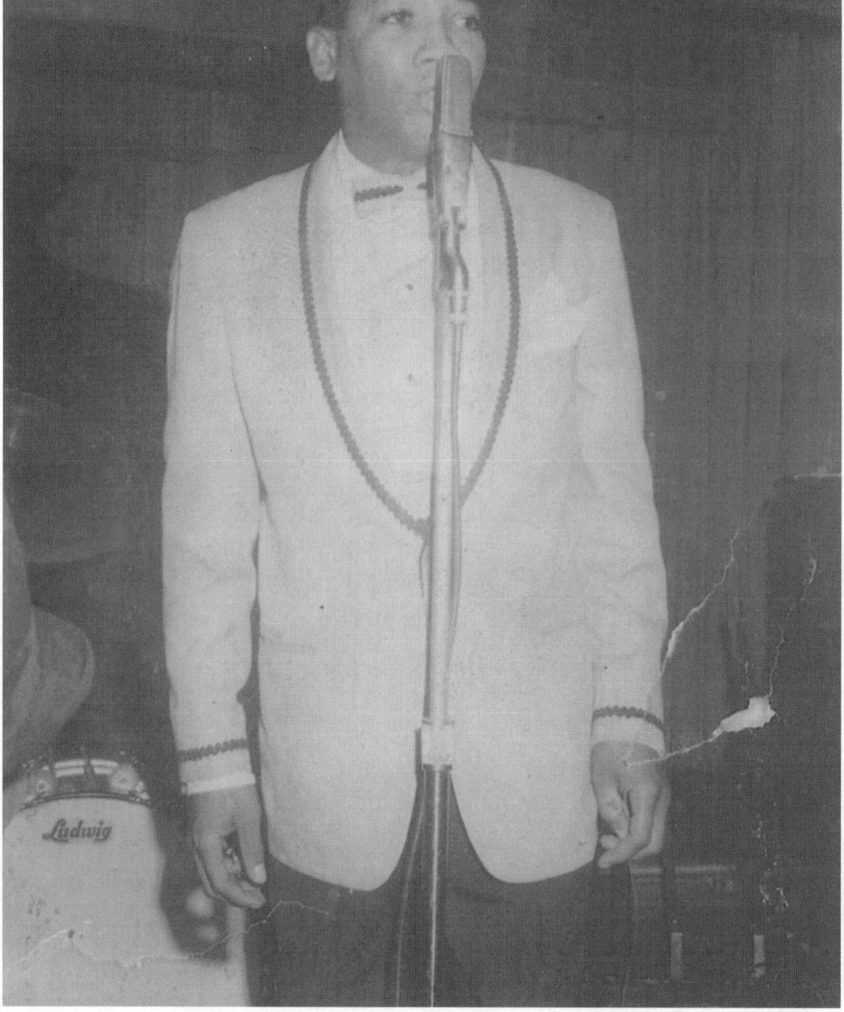
Ludwig

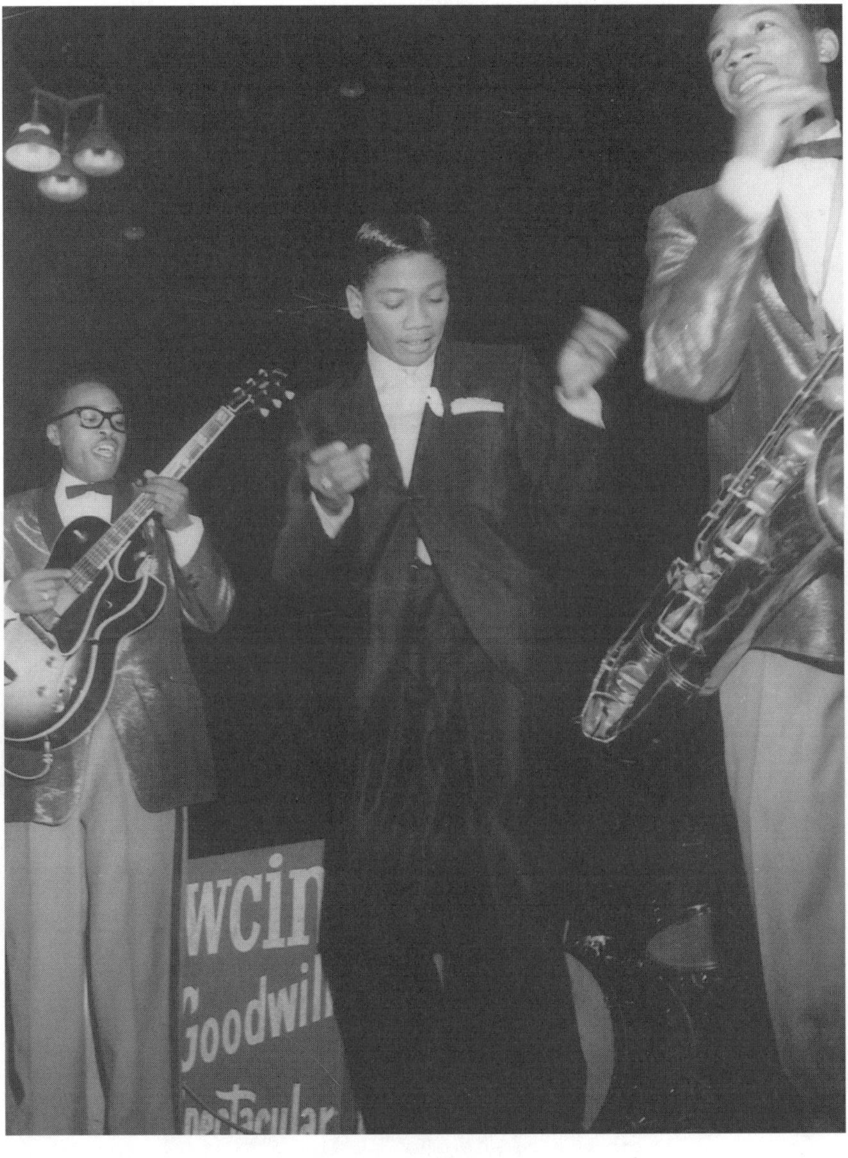
wcin
Goodwil

MEDA RECORDS   MERTIS JOHN

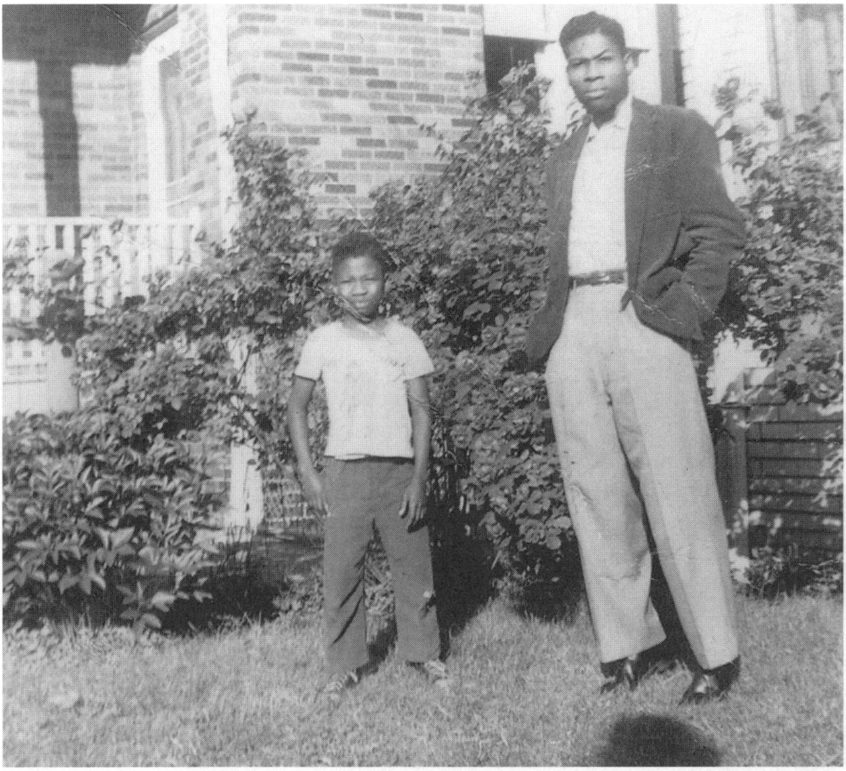

Chapter Fourteen

The Beginning of My Record Company
Meda Records
In the year of 1979, a young lady asked me to record her. I didn't have to audition her because I already knew how well she could sing. I already knew her range, so I didn't have to go through those initial steps before my answer to her was, "Yes, I will record you." We had been members of the same church, Bethel Baptist Church East, for several years. So I had studied her singing capabilities without her knowledge, listening to her sing over the years in the church choirs. Her name is Lorine Thompson.

Her voice is unbelievable. Not only does she possess an unusually great voice, but she also knows how to use it to its greatest potential. You can listen to many singers and it would be very hard to find one who would match the greatness of Lorine's voice, style, and control. Later, when I would take her into the studio to record, the musicians and the engineer would just marvel at her voice.

Lorine is a gospel singer, and she declares she would never sing anything other than gospel music. Although gospel was my roots in music, I had been away from singing and writing gospel songs since I was about twenty or twenty-one years old. I didn't have any songs to teach her for the future recordings we would be doing. I had planned to cut a master on her and then shop it at record companies until I found one that would buy or lease it and release it. I didn't have a record company at the time, nor did I see myself owning one in the future. I only wanted to write for her and to manage her.

The first chance I got I called Mother Dear to tell her I would be recording this young lady who had a great voice. Mother Dear said she was

My Life and Experiences in the Entertainment World

happy about it. She also said it was about time I started working in that capacity of the business. Then I told her before I could start working with Lorine, I needed some songs for her because I didn't have any to start with. Mother Dear quickly said without hesitation, "You don't need to look for any songs, the songs you need you can write yourself. You are a writer. You write what you need."

That was all I needed. Her very words gave me all the inspiration that I needed to write gospel songs again. Up to that point, I was a little apprehensive about writing gospel songs because I had not written any for a long time. I wanted the right songs for Lorine. After hearing Mother Dear's words, I was ready right then and there to begin writing. I thanked Mother Dear for the inspiring spark she had lit within me. She was just being the Mother Dear that I know. Through the years, she always woke me when I needed to be with her encouraging words, making sure that we had complete confidence in whatever we were attempting to do. She handled this situation in her usual earnest and deeply concerned manner.

From that point, I went ahead and started writing songs for singer, Lorine Thompson. I wrote six songs for her in the first group. Then I took them to her and we started rehearsals so that she could learn them and then record them. After we got the songs down good, I called on my good friend, musician, and arranger, Joseph Hunter, to write out the arrangements for the songs. After the arrangements were finished, I took her into the studio to record them. At first, I thought I had what I had needed to shop the companies that I felt would accept a new gospel artist. My shopping was fruitless. I called Miss Thompson and told her that I was going to try something else for her. "What are you going to do?" she asked. I told her I was going to write some more songs for her, but they would be different from the ones that I had already written, songs that were more contemporary. I told her I would let her know when I had finished them. I went to work on two new songs. That's when I wrote, "You Don't Know," and "I Found Treasures In God," two songs that I knew would work.

I was very happy with the songs when I had finished them. I called Ms. Thompson and we set up the time that we would begin rehearsals to learn the new songs. After she had learned them, I again contacted Joseph Hunter and brought him in on the rehearsal. After the rehearsals, I told Joseph that I was going to record those new songs and I asked him to play the piano on the session. I also asked him to contact the musicians that I needed to play on the session. I told him everything I wanted, including live strings on the session. I also told him that I wanted him to write the arrangements.

After that was all finished, I secured studio time. We went into the superlicks studio and recorded the new songs. I chose, "You Don't Know" for the "A" side and of course, "I Found Treasures In God" as the "B" side. With my choice of songs and Joseph Hunter's mellow arrangements coming together with Ms. Thompson's sweet melodic voice, we had a package that made us all proud.

Mertis John

Fed up with trying to deal with already established record companies, I went downtown and secured a license to start my own company. The company name would be Meda Records, which comes from the first two letters in my name and the first two letters in my son's name. That was in 1980.

People Most Instrumental in the Success of My Career
Sid Nathan who was the owner and president of King Records was the first person to introduce me to the business side of the record industry. He taught me who I should get acquainted with in regards to filing the proper documents to insure my getting the rightful payments legally do me as a songwriter. This included getting with my music affiliate BMI and the processes necessary to protect myself and be rewarded for my creative work.

Also, I'm appreciative to him for thinking enough of my songs to accept them and to allow my brother Willie to record them when I would present them at the record sessions. That was the beginning of my success as a writer.

I thank Henry Clover, who was the Artist and Repertoire Director at King Records, for giving me lessons on how to make a record session come together and how to produce a project.

Third, I'd like to give thanks to my brother Willie, who was always eager to record songs which I would write for him, and to also have me on the road with him as much as possible.

Then later on, my sister Mable, who is well-versed in the business side of the entertainment industry, who took up where Sid Nathan left off, after he passed away. She has helped me greatly by teaching me to do things correctly and all the ins and outs of the business and production sides of the industry. She has also helped me in the operations of my record company, Meda Records, and with our music publishing company. Mertis Music Company and its catalog. She also serves as senior vice president and heads up the promotion process in the company.

When I informed her that I was forming my own record company in 1980, we went first in Detroit and later in Los Angeles to discuss how I had planned to move. She was very enthusiastic about the idea and was very eager to be a part of it. I brought her on board then. We have been working together in unison ever since.

As for the studio and getting music together, arranging, choosing, and acquiring the right musicians for the various types of sessions, and even songwriting at times, I have had the very artistic and capable talents of none other than Joseph E. Hunter. He became our Artist and Repertoire Director at the start up of the company. Joe (as he is affectionately known) and I, have been working together in some musical capacity or another since the early 1950s. He has worked with other members of my family as well. He has worked with Mable on some record sessions, while both of them were at Motown Records. Also, he has worked with Willie and Mable

The second side for Ms. Thompson was this record
I Found Treasures In God.

CHRISTMAS COMES BUT ONCE A YEAR

By

MERTIS JOHN

As Sung By The Lamp Sisters
On MEDA RECORDS

CHRISTMAS COMES BUT ONCE A YEAR

Arranged by
Joseph Hunter

Words and Music by
Mertis John

CHRISTMAS COMES BUT ONCE A YEAR (2)

will be re-mem-bered through the year.
this glo-ri-ous day hear the choir sing.

At this time love fills the air

peo-ple are help-ful loy-al and true with hap-py greet-ings the

whole day through.

CHRISTMAS COMES BUT ONCE A YEAR (3)

(3.) Christmas comes __ but once a year brings thoughts of love, __ and friends so dear and what we do for Christmas dear will be re-mem-bered through __ the year.

In 1990 we release this album on Mable John Entitled
"Where Can I Find Jesus"

My Life and Experiences in the Entertainment World

on the road at various times. In addition, he and I have collaborated on several songs.

Raymond, another brother, has also worked with Joe. The two of them have worked on some musical projects in the studio, as well as some projects on big Mabelle in New York City.

The Organization
The first move I made in organizing the company was to bring Joseph Hunter in as the Artist and Repertoire Director. So from the outset, Joseph and I began to work together on our new venture. We had worked together over the years.

Meda had it's first release in August 1981 when "You Don't Know," recorded by Lorine Thompson, was released. The next move I made was to acquire the services of Dan Underwood to handle our national promotion. Ms. Janie Bradford, who is the founder and editor of the Entertainment Connection Magazine and a publicist who is very knowledgeable in the entertainment industry, became our public relations director. Being a Motown Alumnus, Motown's first receptionist, and a songwriter who had written a list of Motown hits, she came in to handle our press releases and publicity. My sister Mable, as I previously stated, was also hired. She is currently in an executive position. At first she served as vice president of marketing and promotion and she was later promoted to executive vice president of the company.

While Dan Underwood was on one of his promotion tours in the South, he heard a singer in Houston, Texas that he recommended I hear. Her name was Lorene Daniels. After hearing her, I immediately signed her. Soon after, we released, "Guilty," with her and she became our second artist.

In 1984, I wrote a Christmas song that I was very proud of. It's a sweet ballad entitled, "Christmas Comes But Once A Year." When I wrote that song, I was writing with the intent that it would be a song embraced by the whole world for many years to come.

It was recorded by the Lamp Sisters who were brought to the company by Joseph Hunter. Later, the Artist and Repertoire Director Joseph Hunter, also brought the Lamp Sisters' brother, Buddy, to us. He had been recording for Duke Records located in Houston, Texas. We released "Keep on Moving" on him.

In 1987, we signed Lessie Williams. Her album was the first released by Meda. The album which we released with her was a gospel album entitled, *Jesus Is Mine*. In 1988, we were able to record an outstanding fellow, Chicago Pete, a blues singer who also plays the bass. I wrote a song entitled, "Why Did You Leave Me," backed with "You're Still The One" for him. You won't meet a finer guy in the business than him.

Our Artist and Repertoire Director, Joseph Hunter, wrote a song entitled, "Traffic Mania." In 1989, he recorded it with James Lawton (also

Our very first release for Meda Records was this record
You Don't Know, by Ms. Lorine Thompson.

My Life and Experiences in the Entertainment World

known as "Baby Pepper"). I took it on myself to do the photo shoot and the design for the album jacket on that record.

Later that year, another officer of the company, a recording veteran, made her record debut as far as Meda Records was concerned. My sister Mable recorded her first gospel album. She put together a fine collection of tunes for the album. One of which, "Brand New World," was written by her. *Where Can I Find Jesus* was the title of the album and the title song.

Starting Meda Records wasn't something I ever planned to do. But I felt at that point, that it was what I needed to do. Thinking back now on how and why it happened, my mind goes back to the time when Ms. Lorine Thompson asked me to record her. I promised her then that I would because I knew her voice and talent should be wider seen and heard. After I gave her my word, I had to follow through on it. That's the way I am. But if it had not been for her asking me to record her, there never would have been a Meda Records.

In late April 1980, I traveled to Las Vegas in the spring. It was a wonderful trip, and it was enjoyable being there at that time. Therefore I was in good spirits after returning home. I drove over to Mother Dear's home shortly after returning, as I always did. I wanted to see her and see the other members of the family that I had not seen for a couple of weeks. We were all happy to see each other. We carried on as we always did. Talking loud, someone on the piano and everyone talking about what they were doing or what they're going to do. Toronto was always on his drums, smiling and dancing. We had a large family and we were sometimes noisy when we got together talking and singing. That was a sign of our happiness. As a matter of fact, that was the family's trademark. After all, our parents had started us doing that many years before.

I spoke with Toronto about doing some drum work for me on some of my recording sessions that would be coming up. He said that he would be happy to play on the sessions. So we both were looking forward to getting together in the studio. A little later on that evening before I got ready to leave for home, Toronto asked me if I would lend him a piece of money. I told him, of course I would.

He asked, "Do you have?" Whatever the amount he wanted.

I said, "Yes, here it is." I trusted Toronto totally. I knew he would repay me. I didn't give it a second thought. He lived in the home with Mother Dear. He told me that he would repay me the following Friday. He said he would leave that amount on the buffet.

"When you come over, you will see it there," he said to me. He also said if I didn't see it and he wasn't home at the time, to ask Mother Dear. "That would mean that I left it with her." Well, Friday came and he left the money on the buffet as he had said he would do.

I did not go over to the house on Friday. When Toronto returned home, he asked Mother Dear if I had gotten my money. She said, "No, he didn't come over. We only talked on the phone."

Mertis John

Toronto immediately got on the phone and called me. When I answered, "Mert," he said. "Why didn't you come and get your money? I left it for you."

"Toronto," I said, "I know you left it but I am not worried about it."

"Well, when are you going to get it?" he asked. I told him the next time I came over I would get it and that would be on Sunday. He said, "Alright, I'll see you then."

On Sunday, I attended regular church services as was my custom. After the services, I drove over to Mother Dear's home. As we arrived Toronto met us at the door, greeted us and let us in. "Hey, I'm glad to see you," he said. "I have your money. Here it is. Thanks. It's been here since Friday." I told him I didn't want to take a trip there for just the money when I wasn't coming until the day I usually come. But I understood him all along. Toronto, like myself, was a man of his word. I never was concerned when he would give his word on any matter to me.

Approximately eight days later, it was on a Monday, Toronto went to work as usual. He worked all day and came home after work at the normal time. When dinner was prepared and it was time to eat, he sat down at the table. Shortly after, he complained of a headache. He said it was a real bad headache. Suddenly, it was so severe he got up from the table and went into the adjoining room to sit down, actually to lay down. Everyone followed him. A large amount of sweat appeared on his face, and then he fainted. My brother Ernest and Mother Dear put him into the car and rushed him to a small hospital that was near the home. When the medical people began to attend him, they said he would have to be transported to another medical facility. From there, they had an EMS unit transport him to Wayne County General Hospital. I don't know why, it was too far away. While he was being put into the ambulance, he awoke briefly. He said a few words then fell into a coma. He was never to speak again.

I had no knowledge that any of this had taken place at the time, because I was still at work. I finally received a phone call. I don't remember who, but one of the family members called to inform me that Toronto was very ill and that they were at the hospital with him. I took off right away for the hospital. I didn't know what to think, my mind was racing. I just started praying and asking God to take care of him. I kept saying to myself, "No, it couldn't be Toronto. He's the youngest of us and he has never been sick a day in his life." Since Daddy passed away, Toronto had taken to me as his father. He said he wanted to be like me. I felt as if he really was my son. We had that type of relationship.

I was the last one to get to the hospital that evening. When I arrived everyone there met me in the emergency waiting area. I began to ask questions. The doctor who was attending him told me that it didn't look too good for him. Then the doctor began to ask me questions about him which I answered. Then I asked if they had given him a spinal. They

My Life and Experiences in the Entertainment World

answered no, but we're about to do that now. I said please do it now. They said they would have an update shortly. When the doctor came back to us, we were told a spinal had been done and that Toronto had suffered an aneurysm on the brain and that he was bleeding internally. That meant that he had been bleeding internally since the headache started early that evening. That was hours ago, since early evening. The doctor also stated that if they could get him stabilized, they would operate, and that he would be fine.

I went to the phone and called my minister, Reverend Carl Hughes. I told him what had happened and asked him to pray for our brother. I prayed with him right then on the phone. Mable was not in the city at that time. Somewhere in that timeframe, I called her and told her of Toronto's condition. Also, my sister Mildred had already called her. Mable said that she would get here as early as she could the following day. She flew in the next day and joined us at the hospital. Toronto was put on life support. All we could do was hold his hands and pray, keeping our faith in God and hoping that he would be alright. This went on for one week, but he did not stabilize so they could not operate. He had bled too long internally before they discovered what went wrong, and what should be done.

On May 22, 1980, my birthday, Toronto was pronounced dead. A memory that's extremely painful for me, yet a day that I can never forget. His death devastated me and all of the family. It all happened so swiftly and without any prior clue. The family had been struck with another terrible blow.

We went ahead and began taking care of the business that needed to be taken care of. That period of time was not at all easy for the family. However, with the help of God, we got through it. Despite the fact that we were all very deeply hurt, we all consoled each other. On May 28, 1980, our dearly beloved brother Toronto was laid to rest. What I couldn't understand, even until this day, is why did he have to leave us so early in his life? His absence from us is still, for me, very hard to fully accept.

When Toronto was about to be born, oddly I told Mother Dear that she shouldn't have another child. I would have talks with her about it often. She had told me that she was going to have another child and she asked how I felt about it. "Would you be happy if I did?" she would ask me.

I said bluntly, "No."

Then she would ask, "Why, Mert?" I would tell her that she had enough children already. Then she would tell me, "I'm having just one more." But that wouldn't change my feelings about it. Then she said, "I just may have a little boy who looks just like you." I never dreamed that could ever happen.

When Mother Dear went to the hospital to deliver the baby, I didn't visit her. I only spoke with her on the phone. After she delivered Toronto, she told me she had a son and that he looked like me. She also said, "I know you'll be glad to see him." I believe she said this to make me change my opinion about a new baby.

When Daddy brought her and the baby home from the hospital, I wasn't home. When I did come home she asked me, "Don't you want to see the new baby?"

I said, "No."

She said, "Oh come on and take a look at him. He looks just like you." I still didn't believe her, but on the second day she was home, I went into the room when she called me and took a look at the new baby. Mother Dear was right. The baby did look like me. "Do you like him?" she asked me. "He looks just like you did when you were a baby." I took a liking to him at that moment.

As Toronto grew up, he continued to look more and more like me, and we eventually grew very close. Later, as he began to go places with me, many people would think that he was my son. Before I moved out from my parents home, he loved to sleep in my bed with me and I was always happy to have him. He would lay as close to me as he could. Later he would tell me that he wanted to be like me. Even on his high school graduation photo that he gave to me, he mentioned how he wanted to be like me. I will always cherish it.

I'm Missing You Toronto

Now, Toronto, the spotlight is on you.
Let me say some things about you.

You were a gentle person, real pleasant, too.
It was always a pleasure being around you.

You got a joy from dancing on stage.
I wish you and your drums were still here with us –
You would be a rage.

Copyright 1996
By Mertis John

To Toronto

Toronto, in you, I lost a brother and my boy
To have you around was always a joy
Though now you're gone, I'll continue to be
Whatever good things that you saw in me.

Copyright 1998
By Mertis John

Chapter Fifteen

The Ensuing Years
Some years after I had graduated from Pershing High School another graduate came up with an idea to have a school reunion. The person responsible happened to be one of my former schoolmates in high school, Orlin Jones. We were friends during our high school days. He was a star on the football team and a star high hurdles champion, too. While I was not on any of the school's sports teams, I was in the Music Department. However, Orlin and I did attend some classes together.

Orlin began to contact former teachers, coaches, and students and organized a team that would get the word out and supervise the reunion. It was a great idea and the officers, including him, had done a commendable job towards the success of the Alumni Association. To my knowledge, this first school reunion came together twenty or so years ago, in 1980. In September of that year, we celebrated the fiftieth Anniversary of Pershing High School. Our first gathering was at the school itself. I attended that much enjoyed reunion. At the time, I saw many former schoolmates and faculty members that I had not seen since graduation. It was certainly gratifying to me to experience that.

The school was first opened in 1929, and some of the early faculty members and some of the first graduating students were on hand for the first reunion. Coach Capp, who was the baseball coach when I was a student and Coach Hadded, the head football coach, were also on hand. School tee-shirts, sweaters, and other items were sold. The event was covered by the press.

The Annual Reunion continues even now, but other activities have been added. Now we pay an annual dues fee and there is an annual picnic

Mertis John

held at Palmer Park. Monies collected from all activities go into the scholarship fund which was set up to award college scholarships to deserving graduates of the school. The scholarships are given after the grand event. I am very proud to be an Alumnus of Pershing High School in Detroit. As scholarships are awarded each year, we term it, "Giving Something Back." By doing so, we're investing in our future.

The Alumni Association's mission is to support Pershing High School in all its endeavors, providing high quality, value oriented, educational progress which will enhance our world. I say, "Amen" to that.

The grand event of the year which I spoke about is a stellar dinner dance. Quite different from our first gathering, the dinner dance takes place at one of the city's choice venues in Downtown Detroit, such as Cobo Center. In 1999, I was invited to be a speaker for Career Day by Pershing's Alumni Association. The Alumni has a plan whereby former graduates are invited to speak to current Pershing students on Career Days. This was the Eight Annual invitation since its inception. I happily and graciously accepted the invitation to be one of the speakers.

I decided to speak to the students about my career as a songwriter, producer, author, and businessman. I must say, we really experienced a wonderful occasion on the day that I participated with the faculty and students.

There are a great number of young potential college students, who are Black predominantly that should be able to continue their education at some institute of higher learning. However, they are unable to do so because of a lack of available funds for them. Besides not having funds, many are denied school loans, educational grants, or scholarships. This situation should never exist in our society. The government on all levels should recognize the fact that every single mind needs to be utilized to its greatest potential. This can never become a reality unless the government wakes up from its naïve position on education for Blacks and other minority students.

The only way to be a dominant leader in the world is to raise the economic and social standards. The only way to achieve this is to educate the masses in the political, economic, and social systems of the nation. A child born in the ghetto who grows up in the ghetto, doesn't have to remain in the ghetto. He or she should be given the right, as well as the resources, that would put him or her in the mainstream of the higher learning process, eventually leading to a first-class workforce of the country.

It is imperative to the welfare of this country that this goal is tackled and accomplished. I have spoken to a number of high school graduates on different occasions who had a genuine desire to go on to college to better prepare themselves for the future. But because of a lack of funds and no way to acquire them, they were unable to attend a school of higher learning. The doors to what higher learning holds should never be shut to any deserving and desiring student who wishes to pass through them. Let us open the doors of opportunity to them all.

DETROIT PUBLIC SCHOOLS

Pershing High School   18875 Ryan Road   Detroit, MI 48234   Phone: (313) 866-7700

April 30, 1999

*ALUMNI CAREER DAYS/SHADOW DAY April 28 - 29, 1999

Dear Mr. Mertis John,

Thank you for making a presentation at Pershing High School's 9th Annual Alumni Career Day(s). We realize that there are many demands on your time and we appreciate your choice to make time to share with us.

We are trying to provide more opportunities for our students to interact with role models from the world of work. Your contribution of your time and expertise is invaluable to our efforts and the student's experience. Facing the challenge of becoming leaders of 21st century has been made easier with your help. I am enclosing materials for our "Shadow Day" experience. If you have any questions regarding this material or would like to participate please feel free to call me.

Thank you again for participating in our program. Your efforts and generosity have contributed greatly to the futures of our young people.

Sincerely,

Ann Connally, Coordinator
PHSAA Co-Chair/Founder

Dr. Emeral Crosby, Principal

EDDIE L. GREEN, Ed.D.
Acting General Superintendent

Keeping the Links Aligned

JOHN J. PERSHING HIGH SCHOOL

A Certificate of Appreciation

to

MERTIS JOHN

For Participation in Alumni Career Days

April 28, 1999
Date

Ann Connally
Alumni Career Days Coordinator

Milton Gust
Guidance Department Head

Emeral Crosby
Principal

Chapter Sixteen

The Changing Face of Detroit:
The Motor City Takes on a New Image
In 1973, Detroit took on a new image. We, the citizens of Detroit, elected our first African-American mayor of the city. That person was Coleman Alexander Young. At the time when he was first elected mayor he was fifty-five years old. He went on to serve the city in that capacity for a period of twenty years, which is an unprecedented period of time for mayor in our city.

During the campaign for his final election years, in 1989 I wrote a song for his re-election campaign called, "Keep Coleman Young Mayor of Detroit." My partner Joseph Hunter also wrote a song for his re-election called, "Detroit Moving With Coleman Young."

Before becoming mayor of the city of Detroit, Coleman A. Young served his district in the city well as a state representative in Lansing, the state capital. Just as it was after being elected mayor, after Coleman was first elected to the State House in 1963, he was never defeated. After he was elected to public office, he continued to be in public office until his decision not to run for mayor again. His decision not to run stemmed from his declining health which eventually led to his death in 1997.

He was always a very outspoken and no-nonsense person who came to be a symbol of Black political power. He did many things to change the image of the city. Prior to his tenure as mayor, Detroit had been a White-majority city, but he opened the doors of opportunity to Blacks as well. He did this first by changing the police department to reflect the total Black population of the city. Deserving Black officers were promoted to higher ranks in the department. He named a Black, William Hart, as the first

Mertis John

African-American Police Commissioner of the city. The city hired more Black officers up to the level where Blacks would be comprised of fifty percent of the department. The same policy was enacted for the Fire Department. Later he engineered a plan where the City Airport, which could handle only small airplanes, would be expanded. This is something that should have been done immediately following the end of World War II, but was overlooked by everyone except Mayor Coleman Young while in office many years later.

As a young boy growing up in the city and seeing how planes began to get larger and faster during the course of World War II, I was sure that at the end of the war, the leaders of the city would make certain that our city airport would be remodeled and expanded. I felt that way because our city was considered to be one of the leading cities of our nation. Detroit was indeed the arsenal of democracy. It was also the automobile capital of the world, the Motor City.

I had a feeling that the city had intended to be competitive with the other leading cities of the country, and I could hardly wait to see this happen. However, I was very disappointed when this did not take place. To have done so would have been one of my dreams for the city to come true.

The plan called for four stages of development. The first phase was completed and now the airport could handle planes which carry up to 120 passengers. The development was to continue so that the facility would build new and longer runways to handle larger airplanes, such as the DC-10, which carry more passengers and fly farther. However, surrounding communities began to balk at the expansion plans. They claimed that too much noise from the larger planes would interfere with their tranquility and add to further pollutants in the areas. Hardly not…I feel they opposed the plan because they didn't want to see the city make that type of economic progress. Without noise, without change, there is no progress which is what we need a lot of.

I commended the mayor personally after the first phase of the redevelopment of the airport had been completed. I also informed him that I anticipated seeing the three remaining phases being completed. I began to use the city airport on the flights that the facility was able to handle for me. I only wish and I pray that an agreement would be struck, whereby the airport would be able to complete the redevelopment plan that we had first hoped for and needed so badly for the city.

In July of 1997, Pro Air Airlines began to operate out of the city airport. This has proven to be a successful venture for the airline. Passengers liked what the airport had to offer. It's close to the happenings, fun, and businesses located within the city offer much, such as convenience. Parking is free and it features everyday low fares which make this airport attractive to passengers.

With the completion of the first phase of expansion, Southwest Airlines began to operate out of city airport with the understanding that it

My Life and Experiences in the Entertainment World

would move to the second phase of building longer runways to handle larger planes which could fly farther and carry more passengers. This service lasted three years, but there were no further developments in the airport expansion project. So Southwest Airlines then gave notice to the city that they would discontinue service at the airport. With the advent of the three casinos and two new stadiums, I feel it's destined to be a boom for the city.

Another huge issue that the city has hassled over for the last fifteen years is whether or not we should have gambling casinos in the city. Some would like to have them and others would not. Well, the issue was finally placed on the ballot and it passed in 1997.

Our former mayor Coleman Young had the vision of casinos in our city many years before. He brought the subject to us more than twenty years earlier. Many people frowned on the idea at that time. However, that illustrates the vision he had for the needs of the city. He stated then that if the city would not approve of casinos, the day would come when it would wish that it had at that first opportunity. He was so right. Many of the city's population has since changed their feelings on having casinos in the city. The majority now favor having them.

Mayor Young was not only a good mayor for the city of Detroit when we needed him, he also inspired other Black politicians and mayors all across the country.

When Mayor Young first took office, our most popular park, Belle Isle, was not being kept up as it should have been. Certain elements of crime existed on the island at that time. But the mayor got it all cleaned up. Afterwards he started the remodeling of the island. Now it can again be an enjoyable place to spend leisure time.

The mayor also designated a day annually where the entire city gets out and sweeps, picks up trash, and cleans alleys, streets, and vacant lots, etc. in an effort to keep the city clean. Rubbish bags are issued by the city on those days. City trucks pick up all the rubbish and debris after the clean up.

When Mayor Coleman Young made the decision not to run for mayor after twenty years in that office, we elected our second African-American mayor of the city. He is Dennis Archer. He too, is proving to be a man for the city. He has a major building program underway for the city. So far, a music building which is an extension of the Detroit Symphony Orchestra operation next to Orchestra Hall, has been completed. Also, construction is now in progress to build two new sports stadiums in the downtown area, side by side. A ball park for the Detroit Tigers' new home, as well as a new football stadium for the Detroit Lions' new home, is going up near the downtown theatre district. What a marvelous sight that's going to be when it is all completed.

Also, in 1998, the mayor and the city council came together with one of the largest home developers. The plan is to redevelop a large amount of single-family homes in an area near the Detroit River. That's an indication that under Mayor Archer, the city is open for new and big business operations in our city. Detroit is well underway to the rebuilding of the city that we so badly need.

People with Their Heads in the Air or Nose Turned Up
One important thing which I have learned in life is this: I have met and known many people who live on the higher rung of life. I want to say this to all people in general, but more especially, I direct this to people who are in the category of being more successful or those who are more fortunate in life.

No one, no matter who they are or what they are, or where they came from, or where they may be going, aren't and can never be, any better than they were at the time that they came from their mother's womb. I have seen many fortunate people, some of whom I know, make the mistake of acting and seemingly believing that they are untouchable…"I'm way up here and you're way down there. You can't touch me or you can't reach me."

It matters not what you were born into or how much you may acquire through life, you can never be anything more than you were at the time of your birth. Surely, we can, and we should try to better ourselves on the social scale in life. But we should always remember and never forget, no matter how much we may achieve in life, we are no better than anyone else. Also, realize that no matter how much we may have to make our lifestyle a rich, famous, or wealthy one, whatever degree of wealth it may be, it all belongs to God. We own nothing. If there is one who feels that what he has is really all his, just let him die then see if he holds onto it then.

Today, there are many people who are in the entertainment field, and there are many in sports who are making phenomenal sums of money. These people should all remember that they are getting that money from the willingness of the public to pay to see or to hear them perform whatever they do. No public acceptance…no money; no money…no star in the public's eye. It is only the public who can make you. They (the public) can also break you. Despite knowing that, there are many, far too many, that are so high and mighty until they cannot smile until they want to. They are too good to shake their public's hand and they are always too busy to give an autograph. Still, they expect the public to respond to them at all times. Now I know about time schedules. But still, that is no excuse to snub people as I have seen many do.

Earlier in the book, I mentioned the late, great, Count Basie and how much admiration I had for him. I watched him a great deal. I admired him, not only for his great musicianship, but also for his integrity, he was always cordial and gentlemanly even when he was tired or pressed for time.

It would be great if those who came up short in that respect could take the great Count Basie's example.

To the Public: I always have time for you. I had better, we're all in this together. We cannot function with missing links in the chain. Without you, there would be no me.

My Life and Experiences in the Entertainment World

Not all of us learn early in life where it is that we are going. I did not. My son did. I wanted him to follow me in music, but that's not what he wanted. He let me know at the age of twelve, that he loved figures. He knew at that age that he was going on to college after high school. He also knew then that he would earn a degree in business. That was all fine with me, but I didn't realize that he had already charted his direction for the future until he told me.

Many of us don't know where we are going until we are much older and have had at least a year or two of college. Now it really doesn't matter how old we are when we find our direction or rightful place in society, just as long as we search for it and find it. God planned a direction or place for all of us. However, it is up to us as individuals to find out in what direction we should go.

There was a point and a time in my life when I found that I was one to work, not out front but behind the scenes, giving directions, helping to prepare others who would work out front. I was to find my rightful place as a creator and a director. I would find my success as a writer who works mostly behind the scenes creating certain forms of art which would then be taught to others who would perform what I had created. For instance, writing songs and then going to the recording studio and teaching them to the singer or singers who would be recording them. Also, working on the recording sessions, producing and making sure that everything was coming across properly. In other cases, writing a play, then later seeing how it caught the fancy of others who recognize a good play when they read one.

After I started working behind the scenes, I knew that I was in the right place. I had found my proper place in which I would find both success and gratification. It has always been a thrill to me, working as I do, behind the scenes. I am completely confident in the things that I do. I feel that I can successfully accomplish any challenge that is put before me.

We all should find what our calling is if we don't already know. When you find it, make it your vocation for it is that in which you should invest your time and your energies. After you have found what you should do, get into it with total confidence. Without being confident in what you are doing, you are most likely to see failure. Failure...that is the enemy that you never want to encounter. You don't have to if you first prepare yourself for what you are going into, then arm yourself with self-confidence. Stay with it and you will never be a failure; you may experience setbacks maybe, but not failure.

In all, I had several careers because I enjoyed doing several different things. With them, all, I experienced a degree of success. My careers included that of a songwriter, a producer, a poet, a barber, a playwright, an author, and an entrepreneur.

You don't have to do as I did, but you should at least find what that one thing is that fits you best and you can be most happy doing. When you do, go for it with everything you've got. There is one thing that I enjoy doing and I want to say here that I have not spoken on, but I do. I've talked about it all through the book but not in regards to myself. It is singing. I love to sing to people. I always did enjoy doing so, and I always will continue to enjoy expressing myself by singing. I get a thrill out of singing to ladies the most. I believe it's because I love to write and sing songs of love, most of all. That is a good way to get my feelings across to the ladies, and believe me, I truly love doing that.

The following are some of the people I met in the business who were very successful and handled success very well:

The late Otis Redding was a singer who recorded for Stax Records on their Volt label. He became very successful with both his recordings and with his personal appearances. Whenever you saw him, he was the same happy, smiling fellow each time. We were becoming closer friends before his death which was as a result of a crash in his private plane in Madison, Wisconsin some years past. I admired the way he carried himself. I was stunned when I heard of his death.

Another successful singer whom I admire is Aaron Nevels. I have not been around him a great deal, but I do like the man from what I've seen. When we do talk, we never finish our conversation. Perhaps we will spend more time together in the future, when we're not too busy.

Hats—I Don't Wear Them
I wore hats until I was eighteen or nineteen years old, then I stopped. It wasn't because I didn't like them, but rather I stopped because I could not find one that looked good on me. It didn't matter how good a hat it was. The last two or three that I bought, I brought them home, put them on, and wore them to the car one time. Then I found myself taking it off, throwing it on the back seat of the car, and never wearing it again. Then I said to myself, it's not beneficial to me to buy a hat, wear it one time only to the car, then pull it off, put it in the back seat of the car, and never wear it again. So at that, I stopped buying them.

Since that time, I've only worn a hat or cap when I was playing baseball, the years that I was in military service, or in a case when it was an absolute must for safety's sake. Now don't get me wrong, I love hats when they are worn by other men, but as for me, since I couldn't find one to accommodate my attire and my face at the same time, I stopped wearing them.

Lately, I may wear a cap when I'm out clearing the sidewalk or driveway of snow when it is snowing and very cold. Aside from that, I'm free of hats!

I visited a hat store recently for the first time since my teens. I looked, and looked, and looked for a hat that would do justice to me, but the results were the same as they had been in the past, I couldn't find one to satisfy me, so I still don't wear them.

My Life and Experiences in the Entertainment World

True Leadership, a True Leader

One of the most dominant leaders of all in this country was Dr. Martin Luther King, Jr. He was without a doubt, certainly the most dominant leader of my time. Dr. King had a dream. His dream has not yet fully come true. However, we have been fortunate enough to have seen part of his dream become a reality in some small degree. When Dr. King became the leader of the Civil Rights Movement in this country in the 1960's, the daily lives of many in this society were very bleak. Seemingly, there was no hope in sight for any significant change.

Being Black in the South meant sitting in the back of buses or other public transportation, even public facilities. There were segregated school systems where Blacks and Whites attended separate schools. This included schools of higher learning too. Many Black people were murdered by Whites and nothing was being done about it. The local court systems seemed to be nothing more than a joke. Restrooms and water fountains were off limits to Blacks, except a few they made available and they were clearly labeled "Colored Only." Others were labeled "Whites Only." Not only that, lunch counters in stores or wherever, along with most hotels and motels, did not accommodate Blacks. If you found yourself in one, you were quickly turned away, or just ignored completely.

Even though Dr. King is not with us today, I give thanks to him for his untiring work that ultimately allowed us to achieve much for our people in this nation. Dr. King worked to open the doors of opportunity to those for whom they had previously been shut.

Dr. King was a dreamer who dreamed of a better life for the oppressed. His dream was to see everyone, no matter what the color of the skin or religious belief, enjoying a full life, taking advantage of all the goodness that God has made available for us to enjoy. This is what his work in the Civil Rights struggle was all about. In his work, he made many strides towards that goal.

I venture to say, if Dr. King had stayed with us (in body), much more of his dream would be realized today. Dr. King was a true leader.

Unfortunately and tragically, Dr. King met his death at the hands of a sniper's bullet that struck him down while standing on the balcony of the Lorraine Motel in Memphis, Tennessee. That fateful day was April 4, 1968. King's death marked the passing of not just a good man; he was an extraordinary and great man who tried to do greater things. I believe he would have achieved even greater social and economic successes for minorities had he lived out his full life. The man arrested and charged for the crime was James Earl Ray, who insisted even unto his death, that he was innocent, even after spending years in prison for the crime. He was also beset with failing health.

On April 23, 1998, James Earl Ray's life came to an end. He died at a hospital in Nashville, Tennessee where he had been taken for treatment of liver disease, which had threatened his life for the past two years. Many,

Mertis John

including the King Family, led by Dr. King's widow Mrs. Coretta King, believes that James Earl Ray was only a small part of a plot to assassinate Dr. King in order to stop his non-violent movement and his achievements in bringing social change in the United States.

Ray's death was a tragedy, in that neither the nation nor the world can ever know what his story would have been had he been given the chance to testify and tell his story about the assassination as he had requested to do on several occasions, but was denied each time. It is unfortunate that James Earl Ray, holding the key to information untold in the King assassination, did not get the opportunity to tell what he knew about it. Now, we may never know the facts about Dr. Martin Luther King's assassination.

In writing about some of the people whom I most admire, I could not omit including a few words about the woman who is known as "The Mother of the Civil Rights Movement." It all came about because of her brave and courageous act. The woman's name is Mrs. Rosa Parks. She lived in Montgomery, Alabama, at the time that the Civil Rights Movement started.

Mrs. Parks was born in Tuskegee, Alabama which is near Montgomery in the year of 1913. Her family moved to Montgomery when she was a very young girl. As she grew up, she discovered she had an interest in sewing. Later, sewing was to be the type of work that she would be known for.

Obviously, Mrs. Parks did not like the type of life and living conditions that Black citizens in this country were subjected to. She had been, and had seen other Blacks mistreated on buses by the drivers. Blacks had to board buses by the rear door only, then sit only in the back. When the bus seats were all occupied, Blacks had to give up their seats to Whites who did not have a seat. Once, she boarded a bus, she paid her fare, and started down the aisle. The driver then ran to her, got a hold of her, and pulled her to the door, then he pushed her out of the door and then drove away.

One day in December of 1955, Mrs. Parks left work and started home. She was very tired so she decided to take a bus. Sometimes she would walk the distance. When she got on the bus, she sat in the first seat designated for Blacks, just behind the White section. Soon the bus was filled. Then a White man got on. There were no empty seats left. The driver came to Rosa and told her she had to get up, but Rosa had no intentions of giving up her seat to that White man. It would be unfair to do so. She had paid to sit and ride. When she did not give up her seat, the driver of the bus got off and came back with two policemen. The policemen put her under arrest and drove her to the police station. She was fingerprinted and locked in a cell.

The NAACP, of which she was a member, was notified of her arrest. A member went to the police station and posted bond for her release. She had to go to court a short time later. After her release, Mrs. Parks met with a group of ministers and other Black leaders of the city one night. Dr. Martin Luther King Jr. was one of the ministers. The Black community was angry at what had happened so they got ready to put a plan into operation. They said they would no loner tolerate this mistreatment from the

My Life and Experiences in the Entertainment World

bus company, so it was decided that until the company was ready to treat Blacks as first class citizens, they would not ride the buses for any reason. This was the beginning of the bus boycott.

Rosa Parks went to court with her lawyer, but she was found guilty. Her lawyer protested the decision and said he would take it to the highest court of the land if necessary. The ministers and the Black community came together at Dr. Martin Luther King's church that night, the Dexter Avenue Baptist Church in Montgomery, Alabama. Mrs. Rosa Parks was there and was introduced. Then several ministers spoke, including Dr. King. In the end, he said they would walk and keep walking until the bus company agreed to treat Blacks fairly. After his speech, the Montgomery Improvement Association was formed to plan the protest. Dr. King was named the president.

During this long protest, many cars and station wagons were used in car pools to transport Blacks to their destinations daily. Others continued to walk. They did not ride the buses. Still, the bus company refused to change their second-class citizen's policy. Black people were harassed in many ways. Whites tried to frighten them. Many Blacks were arrested. Many homes of Blacks were burned. The Black citizens kept walking for about eleven months. It took one year in all to change this injustice against Blacks.

In November, the Supreme Court of the United States ruled that the bus company was not in compliance with the Constitution and had to change its policy. A few weeks later, the bus company complied with the Supreme Court's order. They changed their policy. A year had passed then since Rosa Parks had refused to give up her seat. Starting then, Blacks could choose any seat on the buses to sit.

This was a big victory for Blacks in Montgomery. This indeed, was also a victory for Blacks everywhere. What Mrs. Rosa Parks had done one year earlier gave Blacks everywhere the courage to fight injustice wherever it was found. At that point, Rosa Parks began to be called, "The Mother of the Civil Rights Movement." Indeed she is. I am proud of the fact that she later made a decision to move from the South to my hometown, Detroit, Michigan. She made the move in 1957 and is still a resident of our proud city. I'm truly proud to have her as one of our citizens. I'm proud to have had such an outstanding woman as she in our country, to realize when enough was enough, and to stand up and make such a splendid change in our society. It happened at a time we needed such a change.

Oprah Winfrey

Sometimes the odds for a successful accomplishment seem insurmountable, but the key is always to persevere. I look at Oprah Winfrey, a strong, determined Black woman.

Oprah is a woman the whole world has come to know and love. She is an extraordinary talk show host, an actress, and a businesswoman. She is also a good book enthusiast. Ms. Winfrey made television history by becoming

Mertis John

the first Black woman to host a national syndicated television talk show. This happened in September of 1986. She is also the first Black woman in television and film to own her own production company, HARPO. She had her own studio built. She has starred in several movies, some of which she produced. She is a tremendously talented person.

She is known as the richest woman in television, and is one of, if not the highest paid entertainers in all the world.

Oprah, you are one of our truly remarkable Black women, as well as one of the truly fine women of the world. Indiscriminately. You have touched and inspired millions.

Oprah Winfrey, my hat is off to you...I salute you!

Another Prime Example of a Good Leader
The person I would like to talk about now is one who contributed a great deal to shaping the rich modern history of Blacks in the twentieth century. What makes it even more amazing about this individual's achievements is the fact that it's not a man, but a female using new strategies. The person I'm referring to is Ms. Barbara Jordan. Barbara was born on February 21, 1936, in Houston, Texas.

As she grew up, she set for herself high goals to achieve. After graduating from high school Barbara continued her education by going to college. She attended Texas Southern University, a school which I mentioned earlier that I had visited, located in Houston, Texas. Barbara didn't get satisfaction by just being among the best. Her ultimate goal was to be the very best. She decided that she wanted to become a lawyer. After graduating from Texas Southern University, she chose to attend Boston University to earn her law degree. She entered Boston University Law School in 1956 and received her Law Degree in 1959. She then became a practicing attorney in her home, Houston, Texas. Sometime later, she had a calling to enter the political arena. Her first taste of politics came when she ran for the Texas House of Representatives in 1962, but she lost the election. However, Barbara didn't give up. Two years later, she again ran for the Texas legislature, but the results were the same as the first time.

Barbara eventually began to become more recognized and accepted for her extraordinary skills. She became the only woman in the All Black Houston Lawyers Association. She was also elected as its President. About this time, she was named the Second Vice Chairman of the Harris County Democrats, the county in which she lived. In 1960, she led the "Get Out and Vote" drive in the county. Consequently, she was responsible for getting a majority of unregistered voters registered to vote, some for the first time in her district. She was a strong opponent of discrimination and segregation. At every opportunity she fought against its injustice.

Barbara Jordan knew that her voice should be heard in government. She felt that if it was, she would be able to make some needed changes in this country. In 1966, she became a Democratic Candidate for State

My Life and Experiences in the Entertainment World

Senator. This times he was victorious. She became her state's first Black senator since 1883. She went on to win her second term as state senator in 1968.

In 1972, Ms. Jordan ran for, and was elected to the United States House of Representatives from her home state of Texas. She became a member of the United States Congress in January of 1973. As a member, she was assigned to the House Judiciary Committee. A good choice for her I would say, with her legal background. Eventually, she would certainly be heard.

I shall never forget the 1976 Democratic National Convention. She delivered a rousing keynote speech, the likes of which had never been delivered before. With that speech, she became the first Black person to deliver a keynote address at a National Democratic Party Convention. She spoke at the opening session of the convention in which Jimmy Carter was nominated to be the thirty-ninth President of the United States. She spent six years in the United States House of Representatives where she was a force to be reckoned with. She did not spend a long time in Congress, but she was highly visible in a positive manner all the time that she was there.

In 1979, Barbara Jordan retired from public life, and became a professor at the University of Texas. I, for one, really missed her voice in Congress after she left. I wish that we had more foresighted leaders who could equal her knowledge and integrity, even now.

A Friend Who Put His Career on the Line, But Changed the Control and Rules for Others in His Chosen Field, Thereafter...
I'd like to talk about a man whom I met in 1959, and we subsequently became friends. The man I'm referring to here is Curt Flood. Flood was a stand-out major league baseball player for at least fifteen years. I found him to be the kind of person who would lift you up when needed, a person who would give you positive points on life. He, himself, was a very positive person. His talents surpassed that of being a baseball player. He was also a very good artist.

I remember the encouragement he would give to me when we would talk. He encouraged others also. That's the kind of person he was. He also possessed tremendous foresight. He was a real deep thinker.

In 1969, major league baseball celebrated its centennial. On July 21st, in Washington, D.C., Joe DiMaggio and Willie Mays were named the first and second greatest living players, but at the same time, something was brewing with the game's players. Earlier that spring, the Major League Player's Association had staged a strike over disagreements concerning its pension fund. However, that was very small compared to what was to eventually be set in motion near the end of that year.

In October of that year, Curt Flood who was an outfielder with the St. Louis Cardinals, was told he was being traded to the Philadelphia Phillies. Flood felt that after being a star player for so long, fourteen years with the same team, he deserved better consideration. He had already, back in

1959, experienced unequal treatment as one of the Black players when he then played with the Cincinnati Reds. During that time, the Black Social Revolution was also taking place in our country. Some of our prominent Black leaders had been assassinated. Also, every Major League player, both Black and White hated what was then, baseball's reserve clause which bound one for life to the first club that signed them.

Flood decided to fight the trade on the grounds that the reserve clause violated federal anti-trust laws. In December of 1969, the Player's Association voted 25-0 to support his suit against Major League baseball. Marvin Miller had been acquired to be the Player's Association's director in 1966. He secured former Supreme Court Justice, Arthur Goldberg, as legal counsel for Flood. After Christmas, Flood sent a letter to then Commissioner, Bowie Kuhn, saying he would not play for the Phillies in 1970.

Flood had wide popular support among the players, even though they kept quiet for fear of disrupting their own careers. However, Richie Allen said that Curt Flood was doing a marvelous thing for baseball and that he could not do what Flood was doing but tipped his hat to him. Jackie Robinson also was fully and publicly supportive. He said Flood was doing a service to all baseball players in the Major Leagues. All he is asking for is the right to negotiate...and that we need men like Curt Flood who are not willing to sit back and let the White men dictate their needs and wants for them....

Soon after, Flood began to get pressure for deciding not to accept the trade. Many people didn't understand. He got nasty letters. Flood was a proven talent, his teammate Bob Gibson said. "He has so much talent he frightens you." Well, I was frightened myself for him, after seeing him taking the action that he chose to take. I wasn't sure that he would win his point. Certainly, I didn't want to see him leave baseball at that time. My wish was that he would continue playing. I felt that he had a few more good years left to play and didn't want to see his career jeopardized.

Kuhn's reply in December stated that: "The reserve system was embodied in the basic agreements negotiated by the owners and the Association." Flood however, contended that the Player's Association had never agreed to the reserve clause and that its legalities had always been questioned, and that the owners constantly refused to negotiate any changes to a system that kept players bound to the club which owned their contract.

Flood, in January 1970, filed a suit in the United States District Court for the Southern District of New York, and named the Commissioner, the Presidents of the National and American Leagues, and the twenty-four baseball clubs at that time, as defendants. Flood asked for over $4 million in damages. His goal was to accomplish three things: first, to invalidate his trade to Philadelphia, second, to become a free agent, and third, to put an end to the reserve clause in baseball.

My Life and Experiences in the Entertainment World

On March 4th of that same year, District Court Judge Ben Cooper denied Flood's request for an injunction and recommended a trial for hearing the case. The denial meant that Flood would not play baseball during the upcoming 1970 season. In that year, the average major league's salary was $29,303 and seven of the ten players were earning over $100,000 per year who were Black. On August 13, Judge Cooper ruled against Flood's suit. Flood then filed an appeal.

Gerald W. Scully had also studied the effects of the reserve clause on Black players being compensated for their true marginal value. He wrote, "The Reserve Clause may be an important factor in the racial pattern of compensation in baseball, it's elimination could remove difference in salaries due to racial differences either in the reservation prices of the ball players or in bargaining strength."

On April 8, 1972, a three-judge United States Appeals Court in the second circuit in New York City which consisted of Sterry Waterman, Wilfred Feinburg, and Leonard P. Moore upheld Judge Cooper's denial. Flood appealed again, this time to the nation's highest court, which on October 20, agreed to hear the case. In that same year (1971), Flood was playing his last Major League season with the Washington Senators.

The following year on March 21, the Supreme Court began hearing Flood's case. In testimony before Justice's Byron "Whizzer" White and Thurgood Marshall, major league baseball attorneys Paul Porter and Lou Haynes declared that Flood's case was more appropriately suited for labor-management negotiations and that the Player's Association was the real plaintiff. Flood's attorney, Arthur Goldberg, argued that labor laws did not apply because the reserve system kept his client from playing in the minor league and in other countries.

After about two years of legalities, on June 19, 1972, the Supreme Court ruled in a 5 to 3 decision that baseball could retain its unique status as the only professional sport exempted from federal anti-trust legislation. However, they urged Congress to resolve the issue. Voting in the majority were Justices Warren Burger, Byron White, Harry Blackmun, Potter Stewart, and William Rehnquist. In the minority were justices Thurgood Marshall, Lewis Powell, and William Douglas. So Curt Flood went to the nation's highest court to argue his case, but lost his battle. However, his fellow players would, because of his efforts, win the war against the reserve clause. The first general strike in the history of baseball began during the Supreme Court's final deliberations on the Flood case.

Through Flood's efforts, he, and all the Black major league players, had come a long way. Although some forms of racial discrimination remained in baseball, the fate of Black players was now the same as the White players. In the 1970s, White and Black players would seek out professional agents to negotiate and bargain in order to gain the best possible contract agreement for them.

Mertis John

The Major League Players Association voted in favor during its first general strike in 1992. The strike lasted thirteen days, starting at the beginning of the season. The Black players were in favor of this action, along with their fellow White players. Curt Flood's Supreme Court case was being heard at the time. The following year baseball was changed forever by an arbitrator's ruling in favor of grievances filed by two pitchers in the major leagues.

Andy Messersmith of the Los Angles Dodgers, and Dave McNally of the Montreal Expos allowed the Players Association to file their grievances to a three-man arbitration panel. The panel's decision on December 23, 1973 was binding, the vote was 2 to 1. Their decision was that both players were free agents. Appeals followed in Federal Court. The court also ruled in favor of the players because of the testimony from Flood's case earlier. From that point on, the whole complex of baseball changed. It all started with my friend Curt Flood, his rejection of baseball's reserve clause, and his willingness to fight it to the highest court of the land.

I never played Major League baseball, but I have always loved it. If I had played on that level, I would be very grateful to Curt Flood for his efforts, and in the end, his victory in destroying the reserve clause in the Major Leagues. Every player who played during that period, and all those who came after, owe Curt a great deal in reference to their success in baseball and in regards to their paid market value.

While on the subject of baseball, I would like to talk about one of the most colorful and most talked about players that the game has ever known. That person is none other than the legendary baseball great, Leroy Robert Satchel Paige. Paige was the very first baseball great that my father taught me about. He told me that he was the greatest pitcher in the game, across the leagues. As I became older and learned more about the game, I found his words to be true.

Paige was born in Mobil, Alabama, on July 7, 1906. He started his professional career with the Birmingham Black Barons in the 1920's in the Negro Baseball League. He played with several teams in the Negro leagues for over twenty years, much longer than any other baseball pitcher. He took pride in letting everyone know that through his entire career, he never experienced a sore arm despite the fact he pitched doubleheaders on many occasions. The relief pitcher in the game, as we have come to know their roles today, was non-existent in that day. When the first pitcher went out to start a game, he was expected to finish it.

Paige had successful careers wherever he played. He became the first Black pitcher in the American League when he was signed by the Cleveland Indians in 1948. Prior to joining them, he had already gained the reputation of being "one of the greatest pitchers of all time." He had led the Kansas City Monarchs in 1942 as they won the Negro World Series. When he joined the Cleveland Indians in 1948, he helped them win the American League pennant that year. Later, he played with the St. Louis

My Life and Experiences in the Entertainment World

Browns and finally, he played for the Kansas City Athletics. All these teams were in the American League where he closed out his career in 1965. He was elected to the National Baseball Hall of Fame in 1971. In 1982, he died in Kansas City, Missouri.

I wish that there had never been segregation in sports. If it had not been, he would have joined some major league team thirty years earlier, made more money, and had even more recognition. He certainly did deserve to be in the majors in his youth.

Lem Barney, and Now, the Reverend Barney
Back in the 1960s and 1970s, there was a football player who really stood out among the players of the Detroit Lions. He stood out among players throughout the National Football League as well. His name is Lem Barney. We got to know each other. Lem was such an outstanding player that he was called on to play both offense and defense for the team. His position was cornerback.

He came to the Lions in 1967 and played eleven years until 1978. I cannot begin to tell of all his greatness here. However, football history did not forget him for his outstanding accomplishments on the gridiron. In 1992, he was inducted into the National Football Hall of Fame in Canton, Ohio. Lem is now a minister, and we still see and talk with each other often. As a matter of fact, we have the same barber, Joseph Jeffries, who does a great job. He has been serving customers' needs for at least fifty years, and he is Detroit's best. Lem and I meet at the barber shop on many occasions for a haircut and conversation.

Lem Barney, who is now known as the Reverend Barney, still loves the game and we talk about it often. However, now he has found something which encompasses his life more than being a standout athlete in any sport. Lem is now a star for Christ. Instead of being on the sports field running or hitting or catching for his team, he is in the pulpit preaching God's word.

As an athlete in pro-football, he was a standout star on the football field. Now as a minister of Christ, his star shines even brighter...for God.

TO: MERTIS JOHN —
TO LOVE AND TO BE LOVED IS TO
FEEL THE SUN SHINE FROM BOTH
SIDES.
            Lem Barney

LEM BARNEY   CLASS OF 1992 ENSHRINEE
         PRO FOOTBALL HALL OF FAME

Chapter Seventeen

Welcome Into the Hall of Fame
In the latter part of 1995, I was informed that my brother, Little Willie John, would be inducted into the Rock & Roll Hall of Fame in January of 1996. That was news that made me immensely happy. Then I began thinking: There was no way that I would not be a part of the Induction Ceremony. I informed the Induction Committee that I would be in attendance, but I wanted to do more than that. Then I thought, I will do something that I had done for him in the past.

Then I said to myself, to commemorate his induction into the Hall of Fame, I will write a song. I will also write a poem about him and dedicate it to him. So it was. I wrote a song entitled, "This Is Your Day." I dedicated it for this Induction Ceremony. Then I got in touch with James Henke, Chief Curator at the Hall of Fame Museum, and told him that I had written the song for the occasion and that I wanted him to hear it. I asked for his approval to dedicate and present the song, to be permanently displayed at the museum as a part of Willie's display.

The ceremony was held in New York City at the Waldorf-Astoria Hotel. I set up a meeting with James. At the beginning I presented the song to him. He liked it, so I presented it to the museum for permanent display. I also wrote a poem for Willie entitled "Remembering My Brother" and dedicated it to him.

On the night of the induction ceremonies, Gladys Knight and the Pips were also inducted. The Gladys Knight and the Pips Award was presented to them by the lovely and talented Diva and singer, Mariah Carey who was all smiles and looking fabulously radiant.

Mertis John

On hand to receive Willie's award was his lovely wife Darlynn, along with one of their sons, Keith. Willie's award was presented by one of Motown's favorites, the one and only Stevie Wonder. Stevie Wonder made it clear he was doing it for Willie, not because "both of them were from Detroit and being small, but in part, because he remembered stories of how Willie in the past, had performed at the Fox Theatre" in our hometown.

Keith and Stevie combined for a very hot duet rendition of one of Willie's most memorable records, "Fever."

Other performers who were inducted that evening were: David Bowie, whose presentation was done by the one and only Madonna. She, of course, hails from a city just outside Detroit. The Shirelles, Pete Seeger, The Velvet Underground, Pink Floyd, Jefferson Airplane, and Tom Donahue (the man who invented "free form" radio) rounded out the inductees for the year.

To my knowledge, no one has done what I did, write a song to commemorate the induction of all inductees into the Hall of Fame. I would like to have the song recorded and then used as the theme song of the Hall of Fame. I would also like to have it sung at each opening and again at each closing, or the finale of each induction ceremony. After all, the song was written for that occasion and it should be sung at that occasion each year. It is my intent to commemorate every member who has been inducted into the Rock & Roll Hall of Fame — past, present and future. I hope to do that officially through this song.

Later, Willie Was Further Recognized for His Talents
In 1998, a list of the 100 greatest singers in the world was voted on by 175 top pop vocalists. The survey was conducted by the British Music Magazine, Mojo. This list is featured in a new collector's issue.

In the voting, Willie is ranked in the top ten best in the city of Detroit. In the overall 100 list, he is listed as number thirty.

MOD. BALLAD tempo
THIS IS YOUR DAY
MERTIS JOHN
INTRO
VOCAL PICK-UP
D-7 E- F6 D-7 F6/G C
FROM THE BE-
VERSES
OPTIONAL
-GIN-NING
HE WANTED TO BE BETTER THAN
CENTER STAGE
G11 GOOD AND C GAIN NO-TO-RI-E-TY D- G HE
HAVE EV-E-RY ONE COME SEE IN MY
WANT-ED TO BE KNOWN
C MIND HE
E- ALL A-O-VER THE WORLD SO HE WAS SURE TO
WAS REACH-ING FOR FAME ALL O-VER THE WORLD
1ST ENDING
GIVE IT A WHIRL
G11 C
FROM THE BE-
REPEAT 2ND ENDING
THEY'LL KNOW HIS NAME.
G11 C
C HE
CHORUS
F KNEW FROM WITH-IN
SOME DAY HE'D
D-7
BE A STAR
G6 C
MERTIS MUSIC CO. INC.
BMI
© ℗
1995
OVER-

PAGE(2)
THIS IS YOUR DAY
MERTIS JOHN
A- PEO-PLE WOULD HEAR AND SEE HIM
FROM NEAR AND FAR
NOW YOUR DAY HAS COME, AS I HEAR THEM SAY THE TIME IS HERE
BAND
COME IN AND TAKE YOUR PLACE.
FROM THE BE-
GIN-NING HIS QUEST WAS TO BE ALL THAT HE HAD IN-SIDE
YOU SEE HE WANT-ED TO SING AND SHINE LIKE A STAR
HE DREAMED OF BEING THE BEST BY FAR FROM THE BE-
GIN-NING HE-
© ℗ 1995
MERTIS MUSIC CO., INC.
BMI
-OVER-
Passantino
NO. 1 MEDIUM 12 STAVE/PO 10876

Page (3) — *THIS IS YOUR DAY* — MERTIS JOHN

...had a song in a matter of time with the best he would belong going here and there to entertain now enter in-to the hall of fame he *(fine)* D.S. at % to fine

MERTIS MUSIC CO., INC. BMI
© ℗ 1995
MERTIS MUSIC CO., INC. BMI

Chapter Eighteen

When it Rains, it Pours
In April of 1998, Mable left California for a few days on a business trip that would take her to Kansas City and Chicago. She would also be coming home to Detroit as part of that trip. First she had to be in Kansas City. After finishing the business there, she went on to her next stop in Chicago. After concluding the business in Chicago. She flew on to Detroit. She had spent five days in Detroit when she received a phone call from my sister Mildred who was in California staying at Mable's home. The call informed Mable that her second oldest son Joel had passed away.

Mable then called me to inform me of the news. She immediately tried to get a quick flight back to California. The earliest flight available was a 7:00 A.M. flight the following morning which she took. I told her that I would drive her to the airport to see her off.

Joel was a good singer as well as an accomplished keyboardist who played the piano and organ. He was also a writer and producer and had worked with Ray Charles for a while during his career. He sometimes played on dates for his mother and also played on record sessions. Joel will certainly be missed by his mother, his other family members, as well as the many people who were around him. He will also be missed by the many fans who loved to see him and to watch him perform.

Once Again, the Family Is Thrust into Sorrow
On June 20, 1998, I left home early in the morning which is a regular occurrence, to go to the post office box to get the company mail. When I returned and as I drove up into the driveway, my wife came out onto the

porch and called to me saying, "Come on inside right away and call Mable. She just called."

I didn't have to be told that Mable had sad news to tell me. Yet I asked my wife, "Is it bad or good?"

She replied, "It's not good, it's bad." I immediately went to the phone to call Mable, who was in California. We spoke and then she gave me the news.

"Mert," she said, "Mildred passed away about an hour or so ago." That was on a Saturday, so I told Mable there was very little in regards to planning the arrangements for Mildred that could be done before the week ahead.

Mildred had been having problems with her health for the three years prior to her death, but she had been ill even longer. The doctor had stopped her from working in her beauty shop fourteen years before and her condition was not improving. For the last six and a half months of her life, she was staying in California with my sister, Mable. She called me when I last spoke with her a week before her death and thanked me for some things that I had done for her during her illness, and she told me that she was ready to return home, so I said, "When are you coming?" However she said, the doctor had told her she wasn't strong enough to make the trip yet. Mable had to put her in Cedars Sinai Hospital a week later when she passed away on the following morning. That was just two months after Joel had passed.

After Mable and I talked initially, she then said she was going to the hospital to make the proper identification and to pick up Mildred's personal effects. Although not much could be done before Monday, we stayed in constant touch with each other, going over what had to be done and how it would be done.

When Monday came, the arrangements began to be formulated. It had arranged that her body would be flown back home to Detroit. It arrived on Thursday of the same week. Her home-going celebration was held on Saturday of that week which was June 27.

I began to miss her then and I know I will miss her even more as time moves on. She was a big part of all of the lives of my family members. I'll miss many things about her: her presence around the family, the many questions she would ask me, all the news she wanted to be the first to tell you about. But most of all, I'll miss her wit. She had her way of telling stories of incidents that only she could. She'd have you laughing about it and keep you wanting to hear more. Yes, I miss her, her jokes, and her storytelling.

It goes without saying, the love and respect that she had for me. She told me when she became pregnant. Then she said, "Mert, if it's a boy I'm going to name him after you." Of course I didn't believe her. Then I asked her why would she name him after me. Her reply was, "Because I want him to be just like you."

I said, "Mildred, I'm a junior. I was named after Daddy."

She said, "I know and if I have a boy we will have three in the family named Mertis."

Mertis John

"Okay," I said. Then I said no more about it.

Later when it was time for her to deliver, she found that she did have a son. I asked her what was she going to name him. She said, "You know. He's already named."

"And what is it?" I asked.

"I named him after you because I want him to be just like you." I saw then that Mildred was reiterating her love for me. I loved her for that. I can't help but to always remember. Yes, she did name her son, her only son, after me. She had always said she wanted one child. One son and no more. God gave her one child…a son. Mildred was successful in getting a son and she did name him after me as she had said, for she saw her son as being like her brother Mert. Well, it really did not turn out that way at all for he never showed signs of being like me, neither in character or in ambition. Mildred wanted him to go to school and make something honorable of himself so that she could be proud of him. She wanted to be able to tell people, "Hey look, that's my son. He made this or that achievement. Isn't that wonderful?" Because he never achieved her expectations, she became very disappointed in him. Even after endless efforts on her part and the encouragement of myself and other family members, he never had a desire to alter his life.

I wrote this poem in her memory after her passing.

MY SISTER

She was a sister everybody loved
She was a sister who showed her love
Oh yes! she was a sister who was sweet and kind
The kind of sister you won't always find

She was always there to lend a hand
And always ready to cooperate with your plan
She would want to know if you had a need
So that she could respond with a caring deed

I'll always remember how she used to make us laugh
She always had something funny to say when we were feeling bad
I will certainly miss her, and her stories she just had to tell
She sent me home laughing many times, after a story she would tell

She kept the family waiting to hear, what it was that she had to say
When the family got together, we wanted her to have her say
Now I have but a memory of the times you made us laugh
But they will last forever--- for they are imbedded here within my heart

© 1998 By Mertis John

THE ULTIMATE IN HIGH FASHION

Elegant Coiffures

SMART & FASHIONABLE HAIRSTYLING
MILDRED JOHN, STYLIST.

3884 W. WARREN
DETROIT, MICH. 48208   894-8736

Mildred owned and operated her own business for twenty-five years.

My Life and Experiences in the Entertainment World

My Father-In-Law

At our wedding, my current wife, Verlaine, was given away by her father who then became my father-in-law. She had been married previously and so had I. I became acquainted with him during my courtship with Verlaine. His name was Willie Clark. He was a very friendly and understanding man who possessed a big heart.

He was a person who was very concerned about who took up with his daughters and vice versa. Yet, he was very pleased about our courtship and relayed this to me on many occasions. Furthermore, he showed his love for me in our relationship. It pleased him to see that we were happy.

In time, we began to plan for our future. The first big plans we made were to get married. What he told me then is that I was the man to make his daughter happy. Further, it would make him proud to have me as his son-in-law. We were later married by our minister at the scheduled time which was set by my bride. I became proud to have him as my father-in-law. He would go out of his way to do for you, what ever it was that you needed. I loved him very much.

My father-in-law became ill in 1996. He was in and out of the hospital for the next two years and was unable to recover. His final trip to the hospital was in October of 1998, when he suffered a stroke. After coming home, he held on until the twenty-eighth day of the month. That is the day we lost him.

I went on a trip to Los Angeles and Hollywood where I was on a program on November 1st. I came back in time to be with my wife and the other members of the family for the funeral and the immediate period that followed.

I have lost a friend and a wonderful father-in-law. Things can never be the same without him. I loved him very much.

Chapter Nineteen

Remembering Mother Dear
My Mother
This is a full chapter. It has the fewest pages of any in the book, but it is her chapter. I dedicate it all to her. Of course, it is not the full chapter of her life. I only added to what I had have already mentioned about her in the book.

All through this book you have read of my account of my beloved mother. We have always called her "Mother Dear." Well, I am writing more about her in this chapter.

Without Mother Dear, there never would have been me. I recognize that fact. I couldn't write about myself without writing about her also. We called her Mother Dear because Daddy wanted all of the children to do so. In order to insure that we would, he also called her "Mother Dear." I may add that she loved to be called Mother Dear.

Very few mothers that I know of, or that I have known, were called Mother Dear. We were a little different from other families and that is what my parents wanted in us, to be a little different. As the family grew. Mother Dear also came to be known as Mother Dear to our neighbors. As my siblings and I began to sing, she came to be known as Mother Dear all over the city and the surrounding areas as well.

Later, when we began to make records and travel, that title, "Mother Dear," spread all across the country. Eventually my Mother, Lillie John, came to be known as Mother Dear to many in countries all over the world, especially to those in the music industry.

I can proudly say that I loved and honored her all my life. That is why it saddens me to have to write about her death at this point.

My Life and Experiences in the Entertainment World

All that I am I owe to Mother Dear. She supplied the foundation on which my life was built. I attribute all my success in life to her teaching me the finer points of life, such as a sound, sincere belief in God, morality, and honesty; the need of a good education; also to discover where your talent lies, then get on it, stick with it, and be the best in it.

She would say, "If you do all those things, you won't have any trouble in life. You will be successful."

Mother Dear was a good person and a good mother as well. She lived a good life and she was fortunate enough to have lived a happy life. She did all the things that she had wished to do. God gave her longevity in life. She lived to be ninety years of age.

On January 3, 1999, she passed away. Needless to say, how great the loss is to me. I could never see her not being in my life. She died in California so we had the task of bringing her back home to Detroit. My brother Raymond picked Mable up at the airport as she joined the rest of the family here at that time.

I had always felt that she would live a long life because of the good life that she led. She was one to take good care of herself all of the time. In my mind, I had seen her living for one hundred years. Mother Dear, you came close to it. She lived what she taught us: "Honor your father and mother that your days may be long upon the land which the Lord thy God giveth thee." (Exodus 20:12).

Mother Dear lived in a way in which we had no problem looking up to her. What she told us to do, she led the way in doing herself. She was one who practiced what she preached. That is why I feel that God gave her longevity in life.

I will never forget how she taught us songs she wanted us to sing on the guitar. She taught us poems to recite. She would put us in a circle or semi-circle and read the Bible to us. She took us to church every Sunday. She told us what she wanted us to be. All this started at an early age.

I am certain if she and my father had not taught and directed us as they did, we would not have grown up to be as independent and as successful as we ultimately became. At least most of us did.

The most blessed thing which she did was to turn her life over to Christ at an early age and she, without doubt, lived for Him.

We made the necessary plans for her services. The funeral was held at my church, Bethel Baptist Church East on Wednesday, January 13, 1999. My pastor, The Reverend Dr. Michael A. Owens officiated. A number of our family members spoke of her life also. Two days after her funeral, I drove Mable to the airport for her trip back to California.

I can't say too much about our mother, for she was a mother among mothers. I am so proud of the fact that I can honestly make that statement.

The following is a poem which I wrote after her death in honor of her. It was recited by me at her funeral.

OUR MOTHER DEAR

She came from New Orleans, many years ago
She made Detroit her home-- birth nine children-- you know
She didn't wait until we were born-- she prayed to God for us while still in her womb
She wanted us to be like her--- saved-- and not just live and be doomed

She taught us the good book early in life
She taught us all about-- the tree of life
She had us singing gospel songs at a very early age
She had us heading in the direction of the performing stage

Oh-- she knew from the beginning, what she wanted us to be
Learn your lessons well, get a grip on life-- take it from me
Singers, musicians, writers, teachers or preachers---
Those are the things that she wanted us to be-
A light that would shine around the world, for all to see

Mother Dear was gentle and very cool--
Do things the right way --- that was her rule
She taught us everything--- the do's and the don'ts
She had us sit and listen- as she told us what she wanted

She taught us to honor our Father and Mother
I couldn't be more proud- to have had her as my mother
Today, I'm blessed to honor you-- Mother Dear-- my mother
For there is no way in the world, that I could have had a better mother

By
Mertis John
1999

My Life and Experiences in the Entertainment World

Otis

It is almost unbelievable how the chain of deaths occurred in our family, several in less than a year's time.

The following month after my mother had passed away, actually just thirty-five days after her burial, we lost our nephew Otis who was living in California in the home of her mother and my sister Mable.

We knew that he had been ill and under the doctor's care for a few months. However, we had felt that he would recover after receiving all the medical treatment he was to get.

He had worked very willingly and tirelessly with Mother Dear after she had suffered a stroke. He was there at her side most all of the time. He would feed her and perform other duties as they were needed. He was an exceptional son and grandson as well. His loss will be a great one. Because he had worked so closely with Mother Dear during that time, her passing just devastated him. He had said, no one knew just how hard it hit him. He had a lot of faith, but he began to lose his will to go on after Mother Dear's passing.

We all loved him, not just because of that alone, but we loved him because he was such an extraordinary individual, as well as a very caring one. Needless to say, he was very dependable. That too, we will certainly miss. Otis was easy to love.

With his death at that point, we had lost five close relatives in the past eight months. First a nephew Joel, my sister Mildred, then my father-in-law Willie Clark, my Dear Mother, and now my nephew Otis' death.

Otis was admitted into Cedars Sinai Hospital in Los Angeles on the morning of February 16, 1999. Mable was at his bedside all day and into the night. She tried getting a little rest that night. She had already informed us in Detroit as she was taking him to the hospital on the morning before. I then placed a call to her but she was still at the hospital. Later still, I sent a fax to her which didn't get an immediate replay. On the next morning, Mable returned to the hospital to see him. After she had spent just twenty minutes talking with him, he passed away while she was there at his side.

Mable called me sometime after. I assumed she was about to tell me that his condition was improved. Instead, she informed me that he had passed away. She also told me of other details at that time.

My brother Raymond and I immediately began to make plans to fly to California for the funeral. We were informed by Mable as to the schedule of services. We were both in attendance as the funeral was held on February 27, 1999. We flew to and from California together since we booked the same flights.

Mable was very happy to see both of us when we arrived, especially because our other close relatives in California consisted mostly of many, many cousins. A great number of them were there. Most of our other relatives there had already passed away. However, the two closest relatives in attendance to Mable were two of her brothers, Raymond and me.

Mertis John

In keeping with the family's musical tradition, Otis played the guitar. Otis, we loved you very much. We miss you more than words can say.

Chapter Twenty

Pitfalls I Saw in the Business
In the entertainment world, the world of show business, there are many pitfalls. There are many distractions that can take your mind and you, away from what you should be about - which is the business of making yourself the best that you can be at doing whatever part you play in the entertainment field. Whether it is a singer, dancer, musician, writer, manager, producer, actor, or whatever it is that you are doing in the business, you should give it your full attention.

The business moves at a very rapid pace. One has to be at the right place at the most opportune time. At the same time, you have to be prepared to take full advantage of the opportunity being presented at the time. I remember with me, there were times when I could have gotten other songs recorded here and there, had I gone to the session with the songs directly, instead of just sending them. The fact that I wasn't there at that time they received my songs opened the door for other writers to present their songs. There are always others there at the sessions pushing just as hard as you to get their material recorded too. Presentations are always given more consideration when you make them in person.

The pitfalls in the business don't come because of the hectic schedules of travel you encounter. It does not come from the many rehearsals that take place because that's an accepted part of the business. No, no, it's not because of the many performances that you are contracted to do, but rather, pitfalls come when you allow yourself to get away from the business of why you're in the business in the first place. They usually come when you permit yourself to be distracted by women, liquor, or drugs. Those

Mertis John

three things that I mentioned have contributed more significantly to the downfall of so many in the business than anything else you can name.

There have been many tremendously talented individuals who allowed themselves to be side-tracked from the business at hand and consequently fell victim to one of the evils that I mentioned. There are many of those persons who I could name here, but that wouldn't serve any clear purpose. I only want to make you, the public, aware of what most often causes the downfall of people in this business.

Years ago when I spent a lot of time on the road, everywhere we would go, many women and girls would follow us. At every turn, they were there. They somehow knew the hotels where we would be staying. They were always at the entrances or exits where we entered or when we were leaving. This was true in foreign countries as well. I remember on many occasions when I was traveling with my brother, Little Willie John, girls would approach him and say, "Oh, there's Little Willie."

Then Willie would say, "No, I'm not him, I'm his brother. He's coming out a little later." (Talking about me.) We would have a big laugh and then be on our way. Willie did that to throw them off guard and to get them away from him. They were left still waiting many times. I many times traveled with my sister Mable, and I also noticed how the males followed after the females too. I understand it's a part of human nature, however it's something that we have to be aware of, address, and control.

After many of the shows ended, parties would follow. At each party, there were always many women there waiting for you to party with them. In show business, a man learns early that you don't have to seek out women. They come to you and they are always around. You need to be really strong, disciplined, and always remember what your purpose is, and know that you should only please the women by performing and doing only things which pertain to your image as a performer. Realize also that you are always being watched and scrutinized so you should always carry yourself as a gentleman or a lady. Some male performers became overwhelmed by so many women in their presence, thereby letting them get in the way of their careers. Some careers were lost for that reason.

When you are doing a lot of night club work it's easy to get hooked on drink after drink, after drink. It's always there for you. It's all around you. You can order at your own wish or sometimes the club sends drinks to you at the club's will, as long as you don't refuse them. Some artists keep a high running tab which can take a toll both on your body, which can have a negative affect on your performances, and cut into your profits or earnings. There have been some artists who claim they can't work unless they first consume a certain amount of liquor or drugs. I have seen this with some musicians at record sessions and while on stage playing gigs.

Liquor has played a much bigger role in destroying careers than the first vice that I mentioned, women. Having too much interest in women has been known to cut brilliant careers far short of their potential success,

My Life and Experiences in the Entertainment World

but liquor has also been known to take an even greater toll on careers. It has killed many. It can certainly be a pitfall worth staying free of. Catering to women in that respect can certainly make you a loser also. The third common pitfall that I have seen is the abuse of drugs, but I would rather say the use of drugs, for drugs cannot harm you unless one uses them. If and when you do use drugs, then you are abusing your body, not the drugs.

Drugs, or the use of drugs is the most common pitfall, not only of an entertainer, but for whomever uses them. It's deadly affects are known throughout our entire society. There is nothing that the use of drugs cannot cause you to lose. In many, many cases, life itself. Just as with the other pitfalls in the business, drugs even more quickly, can cause you to lose your career, your family, your friends, and yes quite frequently, your life.

The very best way to assure that you won't abuse your body with drugs and that you won't put your career or your life in jeopardy, is to never use drugs. Not even the <u>first</u> <u>time</u>. Sadly, that is one of the pitfalls which I have seen some in the entertainment field fall victim to. *You don't have to.* Remember, doing drugs is nothing to try, *not even the first time.* Remember also, the public as well as the people, around you love you just as long as you have something to offer them. But if you lose it, they won't want you anymore, nor will they care to be around you any longer. They will consider you a nothing, a nobody, or a has been, which they no longer wish to have any part of.

Lastly, I would like to talk about a common pitfall quite different from the others which I have mentioned heretofore, a lack of knowledge or an unawareness of the business. By that I mean people who get into the business not knowing what steps to take to be successful. Now everyone who gets into the business comes in wanting to make lots of money. However, the reality is a great number get into the business without first being educated about it, nor do they have the right person working for them who will teach them what they should expect and how to go about getting it.

There are some who don't understand what a contract should or should not contain and what is fair for them. Some don't know all that's rightfully theirs and how to get it.

First, do all you can to educate yourself about the business side of the industry so that you will be less likely to come up short of your rightful earnings. Also, put a person at the head of your business who is knowledgeable and who will work toward <u>your</u> <u>best</u> <u>interest</u>. Even at that, make sure that person is accountable to you.

Remember, the omission to educate yourself in the business can most certainly lead to a pitfall which no one in the business wishes to experience.

Establish a Team for your Purpose
In order to ensure you are avoiding mistakes from the outset, you should form a workable team: (1) the artist/manager; (2) the manager/agent; (3) the artist/producer; (4) business and tax attorney.

Mertis John

Today, your potential success dictates that you have working on your behalf, knowledgeable and intelligent professionals.

As part of your management team, it is imperative that you have an attorney who specializes in entertainment business and taxes. You will need his advice before signing contracts, as well as for his knowledge in business taxes. This team is needed to ensure you're on your way to building a successful career financially and from the standpoint of being a stand-out performer as well.

A good personal manager will team you with a good producer for your recordings. The producer will either write or acquire the proper songs/material for the artist. The manager will see that the product gets the promotion and distribution necessary as he works with the record company in that category.

Another area that is vital to the success of an entertainer is the dates that he or she will be performing, as well as where they will be contracted to be. The agent, working with the manager, decides the best dates for the artist. Their working in concert will determine how much work the artist is comfortable with, how much rest he needs between dates, etc.

The two must also know the market value of the artist. This will decide how much the artist can be sold or contracted for to a promoter, on any given day of the artist's career. They should know if and when his value increases so that they can capitalize on it for the artist.

In some cases, the artist's value is lowered when and if he cools off. In other cases, an artist's value continues to escalate. All this should be known and taken into consideration by both the agent and the manager. Together they should always try to get the highest value for the artist. However, there are times when a compromise may have to be struck with the promoter. Then the manager and the agent will assure the artist can work and not miss playing dates that he should work. That is known as "flexibility." There may be times when you will need to be flexible in order to keep your artist working.

Chapter Twenty-one

Let Me Characterize Myself and My Life
I feel that people who read an autobiography seek to find that person's individual character and particular attributes that he or she possesses and what makes that person tick. Well, I'm sure you would like to know the same about me. That's why I will give you these facts about me here.

Well, let me say, using a certain cliché, that I come from the "old school." I was taught to, and I believe in, doing the right thing. I believe in treating your fellow man as you wish to be treated. I believe that each individual should attend school and aim for the highest level of learning. I believe in God and I am driven by Him. I am known as an author. I want you to know that all I have written and all that I shall write in the future, comes from a result of God's writing through me. I can take no credit for myself, but please know that I am very pleased to be in that position. I live it, and truly love it.

I believe in the saying, "live and let live." I dreamed of having what I thought would be the perfect family for me, a beautiful wife and two lovely children (a boy and a girl). God saw fit to give me two-thirds of that dream. He gave me a beautiful wife and a fine son in Darryl, both of whom I love dearly.

I was a very protective type of parent. I felt that the responsibility of raising a child rested totally and firmly on the parents, no one else, not even other members of the family. I didn't want my child to spend a single night away from home. No, not even at the home of a family member or relatives. Spending the night with non-relatives was totally and completely unacceptable even though requests were made on several occasions.

Mertis John

I watched Darryl very closely at all times, especially at play. I asked his mother to do the same. I didn't want him out of our sight. I would take him almost everywhere I would go, even on the job many times.

My wife didn't have the exact same feelings about protecting him as I had. I had the concealed thoughts that someone wished to kidnap him. I had no firm proof of anyone having that thought. However, it was my feeling that I had to protect him from that possibility. This thought stayed with me until he was at least fifteen years old. He graduated from high school and went on to college at the age of sixteen.

I am still satisfied however, that I had the thought to give him all of the protection that I gave to him. After all, no one else would have given him the type of protection which I gave him as a father. I remain very protective of the persons that are dear to me.

I came off the road just before our son was born. I did not leave home until he had passed nine months old. During those nine months or so, I did a lot of caring for him and also lifted some of the responsibility from his mother.

The world is a beautiful place and God, in his wondrous creation, filled the universe with many wonders and with endless beauty to behold. I love nature with its countless varieties of magnificent beauty. I have always looked upon the moon, the stars, and the sun with awe. I still love to gaze at the moon. It fascinates me. I love the great bodies of water. I have always loved horses. One of my hobbies is horseback riding. I love the rolling hills and the awesome snowcapped mountains.

I love the beauty in all things. I especially love the beauty in a song and the musical arrangement of it which sweetens it even further. I love the beauty of a poem which makes it flow and reaches its crescent. I'm also reminded of a very special gift which God gave to man, the woman. Yes, I enjoy also the beauty of lovely women. I love being in their presence and seeing them smile.

I have found that a majority of people get no joy out of going to school. That was never true with me. I always loved going to school. I've always had an interest in learning. I was one who sought knowledge and I knew it would only come by attending school and receiving training, so I was always happy to be in a learning situation. Studying History has always fascinated me and it still does, especially World History. I also like the genealogy of mankind.

I would characterize myself as an easy person to get along with. I'm not one to get into other person's business and I don't let others get into mine. I am a person who loves life and I want to live and enjoy the best life that I can. I believe that I have earned the right to enjoy the finer things of life. I say that because I know I have lived a good life. I have paid my dues. An essential part of my philosophy is to have fun and to be happy. That is why I have always tried to do the things that I love doing. Know what you need and always try to have everything that you need for

My Life and Experiences in the Entertainment World

yourself. Be independent. I have always abstained from borrowing. If you get to the end of your funds, then wait until they are replenished. That is a wonderful philosophy to remember.

Now when it comes to work, I have come to love doing these things: the first is writing. I truly embrace writing. Writing songs is my first love. But then I also love poetry writing as well. Later in life, I found I get a thrill from writing books and plays. It doesn't matter which of the above types of writing I may be doing, I love it all. Teaching also brings me joy. I love seeing others learn.

The third type of work which I love is performing. Even though I possess a certain degree of shyness even now, I still love singing to an audience or performing otherwise. I especially love singing to ladies. It is a good way of expressing myself and I shall continue to express myself in that form. I see all the above as labors of love for me. I am one who never makes resolutions. My lifestyle is my resolution in that I aim daily doing my very best in everything that I do. I realize everything that I do has my name or my mark written on it that says it's me, so I strive to accomplish my best in each thing that I do.

I am proud to be a Baptist. I do not drink or smoke. I'm a married man who is high-strung but at the same time, even-tempered, modest, and intelligent. I did not wait until I became an adult to accept the responsibility of life and of myself, though I could have. I always wanted the responsibility of taking care of myself. That is why I've always wanted to work. I could hardly wait until I could work and begin to take care of myself. When I became thirteen years of age, only a few days passed when I had a serious talk with my father. I reminded him that he and mother had eight children at that point to care for and there was also Mother Dear. The ninth child was born later.

I had a vision even then of earning a living for myself. I asked him if I could accept a job which I could work on a regular basis. He asked me why I wanted to do that. "Are you thinking of school?" he asked. I stated to him that I would always remain in school.

However, "Having all of us to take care of is not an easy task for you. I can help you. I can help you if I can acquire a steady job that I can count on. That way I could take care of my responsibilities and you would have one less person to care for."

At first he was reluctant to allow me to work that much when I was that age and still a student in school, but I persisted and ultimately won. He relented and gave me permission to work a steady job. When he did, I accepted a job washing and simonizing cars which I did every day after school, ten hours on Saturdays, and seven hours on Sundays. The job helped me become an independent person which was already a part of my makeup as an individual. I was then able to care for myself and I was also able to relieve Daddy of his responsibilities as they related to me. Daddy didn't take care of me beyond that point, he didn't have to. I was proud of

Mertis John

the things which I was able to do on my own. I bought all of my clothing, my school books, and paid my way for everything that was needed. He was also proud of the fact that beyond helping myself, I could also help the family members as well.

When I was eighteen years of age, I asked Mother Dear to teach me to cook. She was surprised that I asked. She said, "I teach the girls to cook, not the boys." Then she asked why did I want to cook.

I answered, "It would be good to know how. I would be more independent and when I marry and my wife is sick, I could do the cooking."

After I had asked, she soon began to teach me. I caught on easily and soon we were cooking together. She then began to lay out whatever we were to eat each day. When I would get home, she would say to me, "Mert, I laid out the food for you to cook today. Go on and cook for me." I would do as she said and I enjoyed it.

Years later, after I moved out on my own, I enjoyed good meals every day as I would cook for myself. I am certainly grateful to her for taking the time to teach me to cook. It has paid off for me countless times. Mother Dear has visited my home many times when I cooked the meals. She has said on several occasions, "Mert, I really enjoy your cooking."

I'm not a gourmet cook. However, I do cook well...better than many...women included. I get a thrill out of cooking for guests when they are invited over for an occasion to enjoy good food and socializing. Whether it be regular cooking or baking a specialty, or both, I'm up to it. The last time mother visited my home, I also invited Uncle Jesse over for dinner. Neither of them wanted to leave.

Another thing I really enjoy is eating out. I'm always looking for a first-class restaurant to dine out. I seek out all the new ones to see whether they cater to fine dining as I prefer it. When they do, I make it a point to check them out at my first opportunity.

My advice to the youth is to go to school. Be serious about learning all that you can. Have a goal for yourself. Aim high and do all that you can to obtain your goals. Your ultimate goal should be to stand on your own two feet and to be independent. I was...I am...and you can be also.

My Life and Experiences in the Entertainment World

It is my hope that this book, *My Life and My Experiences In The Entertainment World* will ultimately become my legacy. After all, I lived it. It was in essence, my life. Even though life for me goes on even at this point. For that, I thank God now and always.

In writing this book, I wrote a story which I felt should have been told. I hope that you agree.

Photo Credits

Photo outside front cover:
　　Mertis John: From the archives of Meda Records

Photo No. 1:
　　Inside book, Mertis John: From the archives of Meda Records

Photo No. 2:
　　My Mother, Lillie John: From the Mertis John Collection

Photo No. 3:
　　My Mother, Lillie John with my youngest brother Toronto: From the John's Family Collection

Photo No. 4:
　　My Mother, Lillie John with my youngest brother Toronto

Photo No. 5:
　　My Grandmother, Rebecca Robinson on my mother's side: From the Jesse Robinson Collection (my uncle)

Photo No. 6:
　　Mertis John, In uniform of the U.S. Army: From the Mertis John Collection

Photo No. 7:
　　The first car that I purchased after returning from military service: From the Mertis John Collection

Photo No. 8:
　　Little Willie John and Mable John with Bill Doggett: From the Mable John Collection

Photo No. 8b:
　　Mertis John at work: From the Mertis John Collection

Photo No. 9:
　　My piano…My Buddy: From the Mertis John Collection

My Life and Experiences in the Entertainment World

Photo No. 10:
My son Darryl, God's gift to me: From the Mertis John Collection

Photo No. 11:
My son Darryl: From the Mertis John Collection

Photo No. 12:
The early Meda Records' Family. Joseph Hunter, myself, Dan Underwood, Johnny Griffen, Buddy Lamp, and Ms. Lorine Thompson: From the Archives of Meda Records

Photo No. 13:
Ms. Lorine Thompson, Buddy Lamp, Joseph Hunter: From the archives of Meda Records

Photo No. 14:
Mertis John in his office: From the archives of Meda Records

Photo No. 15:
Mable John: From the Mable John Collection

Photo No. 16:
Mertis John on tour: From the Mertis John Collection

Photo No. 17:
Mable John on stage: From the Mertis John Collection

Photo No. 18:
The first album released by Meda Records: From the archives of Meda Records

Photo No. 19:
The Lamp Sisters and Mertis John: From the archives of Meda Records

Photo No. 20:
Chicago Pete: From the Chicago Pete Collection

Photo No. 21:
Mertis John: From the archives of Meda Records

Photo No. 22:
Verlaine John (Mertis' Wife): From the archives of Meda Records

Mertis John

Photo No. 23:
Verlaine John (Mertis' Wife): From the archives of Meda Records

Photo No. 24:
Mertis John: From the archives of Meda Records

Photo No. 25:
Mertis John: From the Mertis John Collection

Photo No. 26:
Mertis John with a customer in the shop: From the Mertis John Collection

Photo No. 27:
Verlaine John (Mertis' Wife) and Mertis John: From the Mertis John Collection

Photo No. 28:
Mertis John's work corner showing piano, guitar, horn, etc.: From the Mertis John Collection

Photo No. 29:
Jeffrey Kruger and Wife Renè

Photos No. 30–32:
Some of the awards earned by Mertis John: From the Mertis John Collection

Photo No. 33:
Verlaine John (Mertis' Wife): From the Mertis John Collection

Photo No. 34:
Darryl John (my son) with friend, Gregory: From the Mertis John Collection

Photo No. 35:
Darryl John (my son): From the Mertis John Collection

Photo No. 36:
Verlaine John (Mertis' Wife): From the Mertis John Collection

Photo No. 37:
Mertis John: From the Mertis John Collection

My Life and Experiences in the Entertainment World

Photo No. 38:
Verlaine John (Mertis' Wife): From the Mertis and Verlaine John Collection

Photo No. 39:
Darryl John (my son): From the Mertis and Verlaine John Collection

Photo No. 40:
Mertis John: From the Mertis John Collection

Photo No. 41:
Claudette Robinson, Reverend Campbell, and Janie Bradford: From the Mertis John Collection

Photo No. 42:
Claudette Robinson, Mertis John, and Mable John: From the Mertis John Collection

Photo No. 43:
Mable John: From the Mertis John Collection

Photo No. 44:
Otis Nelson, Janie Bradford, and Mable John: From the Mertis John Collection

Photo No. 45:
Mertis John, Mable John, and Otis Nelson (Mable's son): From the Mertis John Collection

Photo No. 46:
Maria and Dan Leighton, and Claudette Robinson: From the Mertis John Collection

Photo No. 47:
Dr. & Mrs. E. Carmack Holmes with daughter Allison Holmes: From the Mertis John Collection

Photo No. 48:
Mrs. Carmack Holmes and Janie Bradford: From the Mertis John Collection

Photo No. 49:
Pete McMullen: From the Mertis John Collection

Mertis John

Photo No. 50:
    Little Willie John: From the John's Family Collection

Photo No. 50b:
    Little Willie John with Band: From the John's Family Collection

Photo No. 51:
    Mertis John with horn: From the Mertis John Collection

Photo No. 52:
    Lem Barney: From the Lem Barney Collection

Photo No. 53:
    Mertis John and Toronto John (my youngest brother): From the Mertis John Collection